SIGHT SINGING
COMPLETE

SIGHT SINGING
COMPLETE

SEVENTH EDITION

Maureen A. Carr
The Pennsylvania State University

Bruce Benward
Professor Emeritus
University of Wisconsin, Madison

Boston   Burr Ridge, IL   Dubuque, IA   Madison, WI   New York   San Francisco   St. Louis
Bangkok   Bogotá   Caracas   Kuala Lumpur   Lisbon   London   Madrid   Mexico City
Milan   Montreal   New Delhi   Santiago   Seoul   Singapore   Sydney   Taipei   Toronto

Higher Education

Published by McGraw-Hill, an imprint of The McGraw-Hill Companies, Inc., 1221 Avenue of the Americas, New York, NY 10020. Copyright © 2007. All rights reserved. No part of this publication may be reproduced or distributed in any form or by any means, or stored in a data base or retrieval system, without the prior written consent of The McGraw-Hill Companies, Inc., including, but not limited to, in any network or other electronic storage or transmission, or broadcast for distance learning.

This book is printed on acid-free paper.

2 3 4 5 6 7 8 9 0 QPD/QPD 0 9 8 7

ISBN-13: 978-0-07-312706-4
ISBN-10: 0-07-312706-X

Editor in Chief: *Emily Barrosse*
Publisher: *Christopher Freitag*
Sponsoring Editor: *Melody Marcus/Christopher Freitag*
Developmental Editor: *Beth Baugh*
Project Manager: *Holly Paulsen*
Manuscript Editor: *Barbara Hacha*
Design Manager: *Cassandra Chu*
Text Designer: *Glenda King*
Cover Designer: *Yvo Riezebos*
Illustrator: *A-R Editions*
Photo Research: *Nora Agbayani*
Production Supervisor: *Carol Bielski*
Composition: *10/12 Times by Thompson Type*
Printing: *45# New Era Matte Plus, Quebecor World*

Cover: Pablo Picasso, 1881–1973. "Harlequin with Violin" ("Si tu veux"), 1918. Oil on canvas, 142.2 × 100.3 cm. Photo courtesy of The Cleveland Museum of Art, Leonard C. Hanna Jr., 1975.2. *© 2005 Estate of Pablo Picasso/Artists Rights Society (ARS), New York*

Library of Congress Cataloging-in-Publication Data has been applied for.

Contents

UNIT THREE

UNIT FOUR

UNIT FIVE

UNIT EIGHT

UNIT NINE

UNIT TEN

UNIT ELEVEN

UNIT TWELVE

UNIT SIXTEEN

Preface

Introduction

The ear tends to be lazy, craves the familiar, and is shocked by the unexpected: the eye, on the other hand, tends to be impatient, craves the novel and is bored by repetition. Thus, the average listener prefers concerts confined to works by old masters and it is only the highbrow who is willing to listen to new works, but the average reader wants the latest book and it is the classics of the past which are left to the highbrow.[1]

This passage is from an essay "Hic et Ille" (This and That) written by the modern British author, W. H. Auden. One can only imagine that if Auden were alive today, he would consider the seventh edition of *Sight Singing Complete* to be the remedy for the situation he is describing. In order to soften the "shock" of the "unexpected," the seventh edition of *Sight Singing Complete* begins with the familiar and spirals systematically to the unfamiliar. Because the ear craves the familiar, the seventh edition uses a cumulative approach that moves gently from the familiar toward the unexpected or unfamiliar. This strategy can be observed in three new features that are woven into the tapestry of this new edition: (1) the art of the vocalise, (2) the art of improvisation, and (3) the art of reading from open score. These three components grow from activities already established in the sixth edition. Vocalises evolve from Models and Melodic Fragments (part B, sections 1 and 2); Improvisation from Creating Coherent Phrases part A (section 3) and part B (section 3); and Reading in Open Score from Ensemble Singing in part E. In the seventh edition, new examples from the past nine centuries were added to supplement existing examples, and others were deleted from the previous edition. Among the new entries are chants by Hildegard von Bingen (twelfth century); melodies by the trouvéres of twelfth

and thirteenth century France (including a *Chanson* by Richard the Lion-hearted); a double hocket on the tenor *David* by Machaut (fourteenth century); excerpts from the *Seven Penitential Psalms* by Orlando di Lasso (sixteenth century); canons by Johann Joseph Fux (seventeenth and eighteenth centuries); art songs without words by twentieth-century composers in the form of *Vocalise-études* by Gabriel Fauré, Arthur Honegger, Bohuslav Martinů, Darius Milhaud, and *Vocalises* by Alec Wilder for Eileen Farrell; an *Epigram* by Zoltán Kodály; a *Pastorale* by Igor Stravinsky; embellished arias by Gioacchino Rossini; and cabaret songs and canons by Arnold Schoenberg—including a birthday tribute to Alban Berg. The seventh edition ends with a reading in open score of *Es ist genug!* (It Is Enough) from Cantata 60 by Bach and quoted by Alban Berg in the second movement of his Violin Concerto. By comparison with the sixth edition, the seventh edition is expanded by approximately 30%.

THE ART OF THE VOCALISE

A systematic approach to vocalises begins in unit 1 (B-1) with a stepwise pattern that descends from scale degree 5 to scale degree 1. This exercise serves as a warm-up pattern until unit 7 (B-4), where a new vocalise outlines linear harmonies of I–V7–I. As harmonic vocabulary expands, this vocalise becomes the basis for modulatory patterns that are improvisatory. In later units, art songs in the form of vocalises (mentioned earlier) help to integrate the complexities of chromaticism.

THE ART OF IMPROVISATION

Working in tandem with the art of the vocalise and embellished arias is the art of improvisation. An example that shows how these activities are related is found in unit 15 (B-4) where, as a follow-up to unit 14 (D-2), which contains Stravinsky's *Pastorale* and Rossini's *Du séjour de la lumière*, the rhythmic reductions of melodic fragments from these works become the frameworks for improvisations. Both excerpts emphasize the same altered scale degrees (raised 4 and lowered 7). At this point in the book, students are not likely to experience "shock" with these "unexpected" alterations because of the smooth transition

---

[1]W. H. Auden, "Hic et Ille," *The Dyer's Hand and Other Essays* (London: Faber and Faber, 1963), p. 100. [This essay originally appeared in April 1956 in a journal *Encounter* 6, no. 4.] W. H. Auden (1907–1973) served as a collaborator with Chester Kallman (1921–1975) and Igor Stravinsky (1881–1971) for *The Rake's Progress* (written between 1948 and 1951) after a preliminary meeting with Stravinsky in 1947.

from the "familiar" to the "unfamiliar." By the end of the book, students are improvising in all idioms—including jazz. The capstone for unit 13 (B-4) is the exercise for students to create their own rendition on the text for "Mood Indigo." This unit also contains melodies by Duke Ellington (D: 1–10) as well as vocalises by Alec Wilder (C: 1–5). The fact that Wilder is able to combine jazz and classical idioms makes his compositional output very meaningful.

THE ART OF READING FROM OPEN SCORE

Ensemble singing in unfamiliar clefs, or as Auden might say "unexpected" clefs, is a necessary discipline for the complete musician. Learning to read in open score offers numerous advantages, such as strengthening intervallic reading, setting the stage for transposition, and helping students to hear orchestral scores with their "eyes." Clef reading is introduced as an exercise in ensemble singing—at first with two lines written in the soprano clef in an imitative texture. It is expected that students will become conversant with three of the C clefs: soprano, alto, and tenor .

"Hearing music" with one's "eyes" has served as the purpose of *Sight Singing Complete* since the first edition in 1965. In order to reach this goal, the sequence of events is designed to help students develop the aural skills that will enable them to reverse the compositional process of sound into symbol to one of symbol into sound. Just as painters speak of the "thinking eye" (Klee), playwrights and poets of the "mind's eye" (Shakespeare), and psychologists of the "soul's eye," musicians are trained to develop a "hearing eye." For only when students are able to translate musical symbols from the concrete level of musical notation into sounds will they be able to approximate the abstract musical ideas that the composer was trying to communicate in the first place. The task of observing a musical score with thoughtful and hearing eyes is the most significant outcome of the four-semester sequence of courses for which this textbook is designed.

The idea of replaying a work of art in one's mind is not unique to music. For example, a scholar of Elizabethan drama encourages the reader of a play by Shakespeare "to rehearse the play in his [or her] mind, considering the text in detail as an actor would, hearing and seeing each moment."[2] The student of music has precisely the same goal: to be able to rehearse the musical

score in his or her mind, considering the musical notation in detail as a conductor, performer, or composer would—hearing and seeing each moment.

To the Student

Helpful Strategies

Sight singing is one of the most practical means that students have of demonstrating to their instructors the progress they are making in "hearing" the notation they are "seeing." For this reason, various strategies exist to help students improve their aural skills.

1. **Syllables or numbers.** Learn thoroughly whatever syllable or numbering system your instructor recommends. To take the guesswork out of sight singing, it is important to "know" the scale degree of all melody notes and to communicate that information to your instructor—as well as to yourself.

2. **Intervals.** Knowing what E sounds like when you are presently singing C is something to get accustomed to. At first it may be difficult, but when you learn that from C to E is the same distance as from F to A or G to B, your problem is diminished considerably. Learning to sing intervals (distance between pitches) is an absolute must.

3. **Familiarity with the scale.** Figure out the key of each melody and sing the scale before attacking the melody itself.

4. **Reference tones.** Isolate the 1st, 3rd, and 5th scale degrees and sing them until memorized. Then, for a while at least, circle all 1st, 3rd, and 5th scale degrees in the melody. These are called reference tones.

5. **The tonic note.** You should be able to pause anywhere in a melody and sing the tonic (1st scale degree) pitch immediately. Try it a few times just to make sure you can do it.

6. **"Hearing" what you are "seeing."** Practice scanning melodies—thinking (rather than singing) what each pitch sounds like. The sooner you can do this, the closer you will be to developing a "hearing eye."

7. **Steady tempo.** Avoid starts and stops in sight singing. Doing so means that the tempo you selected may be too fast—your voice gets ahead of your mind.

8. **Rhythm.** Trying to figure out the next pitch and rhythm at the same time may be overwhelming at first. Before singing, tap out the rhythm of the entire melody. This "divide and conquer" technique will help considerably, and you will soon be able to coordinate both.

---

[2]Robert Hapgood, "Shakespeare and the Included Spectator" (commentary on John Russell Brown, "Laughter in the Last Plays," *Shakespeare's Plays in Performance* [London, 1967] In *Reinterpretations of Elizabethan Drama,* edited by Norman Rabkin, p. 133. New York: Columbia University Press, 1969). The essay was also cited in Michael Cohen, *Hamlet in My Mind's Eye.* Athens and London: University of Georgia Press, 1989.

To the Instructor

Special to this Seventh Edition

This new edition contains the following revisions:

1. **The Art of the Vocalise**
   - Incorporated in part B, section 4 (Improvisation) in units 7–12
   - Art songs without words by twentieth-century composers in the form of vocalises (Units 11–13C, 12D, 14–15D)

2. **The Art of Improvisation** (units 1–16, part B, section 4: Improvisation)

3. **The Art of Reading from Open Score** (part E, section 2: Ensemble Singing in Unfamiliar Clefs)

4. **Cabaret Songs** by Arnold Schoenberg (unit 14C)

5. **Additional melodies** interspersed with existing material throughout the book, including selections from early musical sources of the twelfth, thirteenth, and fourteenth centuries

6. **Additional contrapuntal works (primarily canonic)** in part E, section 1, Ensemble Singing in Familiar Clefs)

7. **Conducting patterns** designed by Dennis Glocke, Director of Concert Bands at the Penn State School of Music

Format of the Text

The text is divided into sixteen units, and, except for the last unit, in which parts C and D are merged, each contains five parts: A, B, C, D, E. Each part constitutes a track, or procedure, that is developed throughout the sixteen units.

A: RHYTHM

Each unit (except for unit 16) begins with rhythm modules that are then combined into phrases. Students are asked to create coherent phrases from the modules that they have just learned. Although rhythm syllables are not provided in this edition, it is strongly recommended that a system be adopted. Conducting patterns, designed by Dennis Glocke, Director of Concert Bands at the Penn State School of Music, are given for cut time and common time.

B: MODELS AND MELODIC FRAGMENTS FOR INTERVAL SINGING

This part aims to provide students with melodic patterns derived from music literature. Initially, the focus is on hearing and singing before reading, so that students will become familiar with melodic patterns aurally before they are asked to read them in notation. The process of melodic fragmentation serves a number of purposes. The brevity of each fragment (at least in the earlier units) allows students to focus on the specific musical element or elements of the given harmonies. Of necessity, the melodic fragments in the later units become longer than those of the earlier ones because the "vocabulary" is more complicated in chromatic and atonal structures.

In section 3 of part B, students are asked to create coherent melodies on the basis of the melodic fragments they have just learned. (To give students the experience of reading through as many of the key signatures represented in the circle of 5ths as possible, an attempt is made to systematically introduce new key signatures.)

In section 4 of part B, students are introduced to the art of improvisation; vocalise exercises are incorporated into this section in units 7–12.

C: SHORTER AND EASIER MELODIES TO BE SUNG AT PERFORMANCE TEMPO

This part provides an opportunity for students to test their sight singing skills for continuity, accuracy, and musicality. These melodies are shorter, contain few problem intervals or rhythms, require little or no preparation, and are intended to be sung at sight on the first attempt.

D: MELODIES FOR MORE COMPREHENSIVE STUDY

Part D of units 1–14 are made up entirely of tonal melodies, lending themselves quite appropriately to solfeggio, or number systems. Because the materials in units 15 and 16 are more contemporary, systems such as "neutral syllable," chromatic fixed-Do, or integers 0–11 are more appropriate. (Notice that in unit 16, sections C and D are merged.)

E: ENSEMBLE EXCERPTS

Musical excerpts for ensemble singing in familiar and unfamiliar clefs are greatly expanded in this edition to provide students with appropriate experiences for concentration and for score reading with C clefs.

The Available Systems

Most instructors who have taught sight singing for years have either chosen or developed a system with which they feel comfortable. Those who are teaching the course for the first time may be interested in the variety of approaches that are available:

Moveable Do. In one "moveable do" system, the tonic pitch is do in major and minor keys; in the other system, the tonic pitch of minor keys is represented by la.

Fixed Do. Do is always the same note (usually C) regardless of the key. One "fixed do" system uses only seven syllables regardless of chromatic changes; in the other system, chromatic changes are accounted for (chromatic "fixed do").

Moveable Numbers. Similar in design to moveable do, numbers (most often 1–7) are substituted for the solfeggio syllables. The tonic note becomes "1."

Fixed Numbers. A system similar to chromatic fixed do, "0" is always the same pitch class (usually C).

SOME MOVEABLE AND FIXED SYSTEMS IN MAJOR KEYS

G-Major Scale	G	A	B	C	D	E	F♯	G
Seven-syllable moveable Do	Do	Re	Mi	Fa	Sol	La	Ti	Do
Seven-syllable fixed Do	Sol	La	Ti	Do	Re	Mi	Fa	Sol
Seven-number moveable system	1	2	3	4	5	6	7	1

SOME MOVEABLE SYSTEMS FOR MINOR KEYS

G-Harmonic Minor Scale	G	A	B♭	C	D	E♭	F♯	G
La-based minor	La	Ti	Do	Re	Mi	Fa	Si	La
Do-based minor	Do	Re	Me	Fa	Sol	Le	Ti	Do
One-based minor	1	2	3	4	5	6	7	1

TWELVE-SYLLABLE OR NUMBER SYSTEMS

The use of 12 symbols makes possible a label for all pitch classes of the octave. Some examples are:

G-Major Scale	G	(G♯)	A	(A♯)	B	C	(C♯)	D	(D♯)	E	(E♯)	F♯
Twelve-tone fixed Do	†Sol	Si	La	Li	Ti	Do	Di	Re	Ri	Mi	Mis	Fi
Twelve-tone fixed numbers	7	8	9	10	11	0	1	2	3	4	5	6

†Descending order is: Sol Se Fa Mi Me Re Ra Do Ti Te La Le Sol

Acknowledgments

On the occasion of this seventh edition of *Sight Singing Complete,* I wish to express my warmest gratitude to Bruce Benward who initiated this text in 1965 and who generously invited me to join him starting with the fifth edition. He was a valued mentor during my graduate student days at the University of Wisconsin-Madison and I am immensely grateful to him for our pedagogical collaborations. Bruce's wife, Gene, who died in 2004, was also a partner in assisting with the musical examples in the early editions.

I also wish to acknowledge the love and devotion of my late parents, Bernard M. and Emily J. Carr. They always encouraged me in my life's work, and they continue to be my guiding lights. In their absence, their son, Bernard T. Carr, has been most attentive to his sister and for this I am extremely grateful. My brother, my sister-in-law, Brenda, members of their family, and my cousin Joan form a powerful support network together with Cathy and Bill Anderson, Anne and Michael Lescanic, and Matthew T. Laffey, OSB.

I am thankful to my students and colleagues and to those executives who administer the School of Music and the College of Arts and Architecture at The Pennsylvania State University for their friendliness and for their never-failing enthusiasm for my work. Dennis Glocke, Director of Concert Bands at Penn State, provided me with elegant conducting patterns. Marylène Dosse, Distinguished Professor of Piano, was generous with her time in approaching a French publisher about permissions. Other Penn State colleagues assisted with some of the poetic translations of titles: Richard D. Green, Marica S. Tacconi, and Charles D. Youmans, together with Lynn E. Palermo of Susquehanna University and Julia Kreinen of the Hebrew University of Jerusalem. Severine Neff of the University of North Carolina-Chapel Hill assisted with the interpretation of the Schoenberg canon that appears in unit 15. I benefited from having Amanda L. Maple, head of the Arts and Humanities Library of The Pennsylvania State University, and members of her staff and of Inter-Library Loan Borrowing as colleagues.

Phillip M. Torbert assisted in the final design of the cover.

Finally, I wish to express my gratitude to the following reviewers who provided valuable input to the proposal that resulted in the seventh edition:

Thomas W. Acord
California State University Hayward

John Bleuel
State University of West Georgia

Claire Boge
Miami University

Teresa Davidian
Tarleton State University

Warren Gooch
Truman State University

Earl Holt
North Harris College

Cherise D. Leiter
Metropolitan State College of Denver

Larry L. Stukenholtz
St. Louis Community College

Eleanor Trawick
Ball State University

I also want to thank the editors for the extraordinary care with which they treated me and my manuscript: Chris Freitag and Melody Marcus, sponsoring editors; Beth Ebenstein, editorial assistant; Beth Baugh, developmental editor; Anne Wallingford, permissions coordinator; Barbara Hacha, manuscript editor; Holly Paulsen, project manager; Cassandra Chu, design manager; and James L. Zychowicz and Mary Ann Fraley of A-R Editions, responsible for the encoding of the musical notation. Each level of the process that resulted in the publication of this textbook was characterized by professionalism, humanism, and optimism.

UNIT ONE

A Rhythm—Simple Meter: One-, Two-, and Three-Beat Values

SECTION 1. Modules in Simple Meter

Using a neutral syllable, sing the patterns in each of the given modules. Begin by repeating each module several times. Then treat the successive modules as a continuous exercise.

Notice that the values of the notes and rests in these modules encompass one, two, or three beats. The quarter note represents the beat in meters such as $[\frac{2}{4}]$, $[\frac{3}{4}]$, and $[\frac{4}{4}]$; the eighth note in $[\frac{3}{8}]$ and $[\frac{4}{8}]$; the sixteenth note in $[\frac{4}{16}]$; the half note in $[\frac{4}{2}]$; the whole note in $[\frac{3}{1}]$; and so on. In subsequent chapters you will learn how to divide beats. This process will help you understand the difference between simple and compound meter.

For a complete explanation of the differences between simple meter and compound meter, see Benward and Saker, *Music in Theory and Practice,* vol. 1 (7th ed.), p. 10.

Use the conducting patterns shown below, if your instructor recommends you do so.

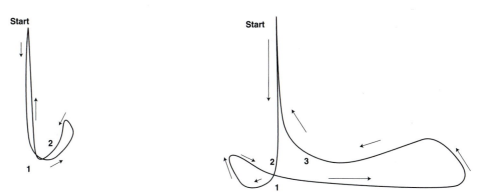

Credit: All conducting patterns in this edition are designed by Dennis Glocke, Director of Concert Bands at The Pennsylvania State University School of Music.

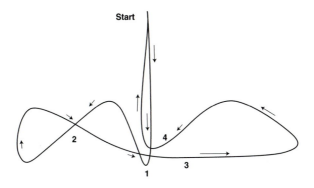

1

SECTION 2. Phrases in Simple Meter

Eventually, you will learn to internalize the beat, but in the early stages of learning to read rhythms you can use a number of procedures:

1. Clap the meter and sing the rhythm (use a neutral syllable or the system of rhythm syllables recommended by your instructor).
2. Sing the meter and clap the rhythm.
3. Tap the meter with one hand and the rhythm with the other.
4. Half the class taps the meter while the other half claps the rhythm.

SECTION 3. Creating a Coherent Phrase in Simple Meter

Return to section 1 and select three or four rhythm modules. Place them in an order that would create a coherent four-measure phrase. Here is an example based on modules 11, 4, and 3:

Write your solution on the following line:

Use a neutral syllable to sing your phrase and have your classmates identify which modules you selected and the order in which you sang them. At some future date, return to this phrase and add the melodic dimension.

B Diatonic Models and Melodic Fragments for Interval Singing: M2 and m2

SECTION 1. Diatonic Models

(A) VOCALISE DESCENDING FROM $\hat{5}$ TO $\hat{1}$

Neighboring tone figures in combination with passing tone figures outline a descending line from scale degrees 5 to 1. Exercises 1–3 combine neighboring and passing tone figures to fill in a descending line from scale degrees 5 to 1 in major and minor. These passages (or *vocalises*) may be used as a way to establish the key for tonal exercises and melodies throughout the book.

Procedure

MODELS 1–3

Step 1. Your instructor sings or plays figure 1 (major) as a means of establishing the key.

Step 2. Repeat (sing) the same figure your instructor provides in step 1.

Step 3. For additional practice, follow the same procedure in each major key by moving down a perfect 5th (or up a perfect 4th), first to F major, then to B♭, E♭, and so on. See the following model:

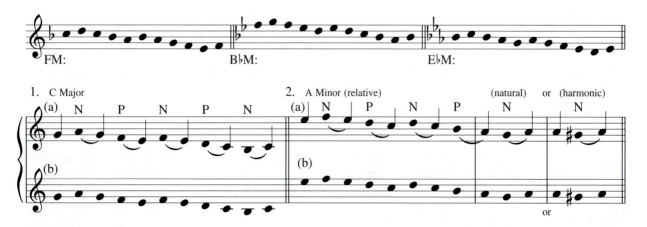

3. C Minor (parallel)   (natural)   or   (harmonic)

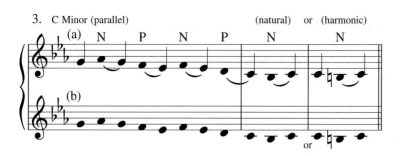

(B) VOCALISE DESCENDING FROM $\hat{1}$ TO $\hat{5}$ AND ASCENDING FROM $\hat{5}$ TO $\hat{1}$

Double neighboring tone figures at cadential points will help you confirm the tonic of a key. This model will be useful to you in writing creative exercises. As with the previous vocalise, this passage may be used as a way to establish the key for tonal exercises and melodies throughout the book.

Procedure

MODEL 4

Follow the same procedure for singing this vocalise in different keys down a 5th (or up a 4th).

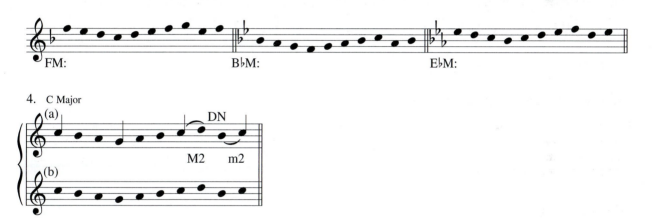

FM: BbM: EbM:

4. C Major

(a)

DN

M2   m2

(b)

(C) VOCALISE ASCENDING FROM $\hat{1}$ TO $\hat{5}$ AND DESCENDING FROM $\hat{5}$ TO $\hat{1}$

Procedure

MODEL 5

Follow the same procedure for singing this vocalise in different keys down a 5th (or up a 4th).

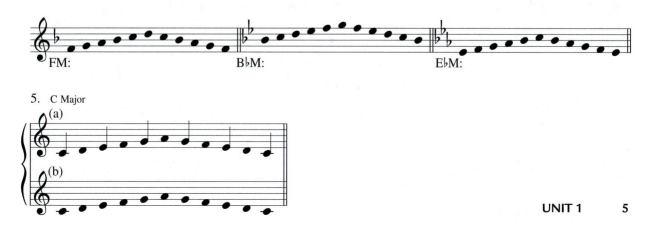

FM: BbM: EbM:

5. C Major

(a)

(b)

SECTION 2. Melodic Fragments in F Major

These melodic fragments are taken from music literature for the purpose of providing a musical context for the intervals M2 and m2. Examples of neighboring, passing, and double neighboring tones occur in abundance.

Procedure

1. Your instructor establishes the key for each of the fragments, using one of the *vocalises* taught in exercises 1, 2, 3, 4, or 5 transposed to the appropriate pitch level.
2. Sing the following excerpts and identify neighboring, passing, and double neighboring tone figures as well as intervals.

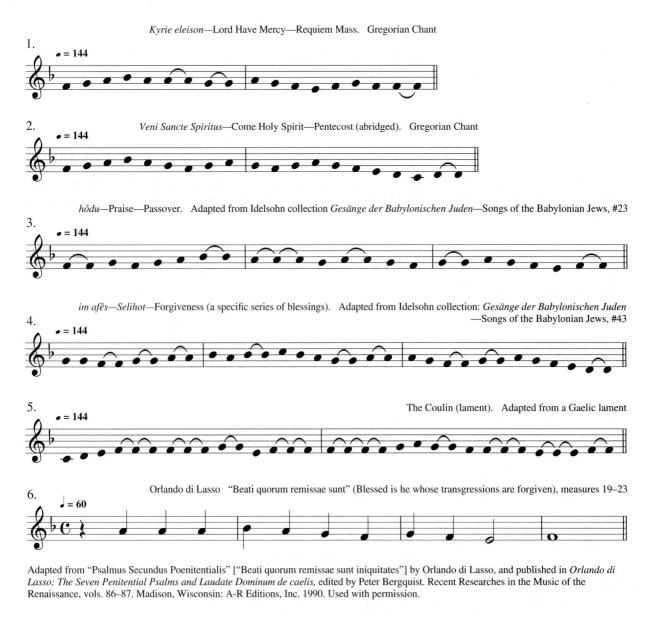

1. *Kyrie eleison*—Lord Have Mercy—Requiem Mass. Gregorian Chant

2. *Veni Sancte Spiritus*—Come Holy Spirit—Pentecost (abridged). Gregorian Chant

3. *hôdu*—Praise—Passover. Adapted from Idelsohn collection *Gesänge der Babylonischen Juden*—Songs of the Babylonian Jews, #23

4. *im afês*—Selihot—Forgiveness (a specific series of blessings). Adapted from Idelsohn collection: *Gesänge der Babylonischen Juden*—Songs of the Babylonian Jews, #43

5. The Coulin (lament). Adapted from a Gaelic lament

6. Orlando di Lasso "Beati quorum remissae sunt" (Blessed is he whose transgressions are forgiven), measures 19–23

Adapted from "Psalmus Secundus Poenitentialis" ["Beati quorum remissae sunt iniquitates"] by Orlando di Lasso, and published in *Orlando di Lasso: The Seven Penitential Psalms and Laudate Dominum de caelis,* edited by Peter Bergquist. Recent Researches in the Music of the Renaissance, vols. 86–87. Madison, Wisconsin: A-R Editions, Inc. 1990. Used with permission.

7. Orlando di Lasso "Domine, ne in furore" (Oh Lord do not rebuke me), measures 33–39

Adapted from "Psalmus Primus Poenitentialis" ["Domine, ne in furore tuo"] by Orlando di Lasso, and published in *Orlando di Lasso: The Seven Penitential Psalms and Laudate Dominum de caelis,* edited by Peter Bergquist. Recent Researches in the Music of the Renaissance, vols. 86–87. Madison, Wisconsin: A-R Editions, Inc. 1990. Used with permission.

Adapted from a song by Charles E. Graaf, composed in the Hague, 1766; the basis for Mozart's Eight Variations, K. Anh. 208 (24), meas. 1–4.

8.

Adapted from "Ah, vous dirai-je, Maman" (Ah! I will Tell You, Mama) composed in Paris, 1778; the basis for Mozart's Twelve Variations, K. 265(300e), meas. 1–8.

9.

10.

J.S. Bach, *Sinfonia 13*, BWV 799 (transposed), meas. 13–18.

SECTION 3. Creating a Coherent Phrase

Return to section 2 and select two or three segments of melodic fragments 1–5. Place them in an order that would create a coherent chant. Here is an example based on the first and last segments of fragment 4 and the first segment of fragment 5.

SECTION 4. Improvisation

The best way to learn the "art of improvisation" is to restrict yourself to the metric and melodic patterns that you have already experienced in unit 1.

Here are some guidelines to ensure a logical outcome:

1. Establish a rhythmic framework (and/or)
2. Establish a tonal outline

For example:

1. Rhythmic framework:

2. Tonal outline:

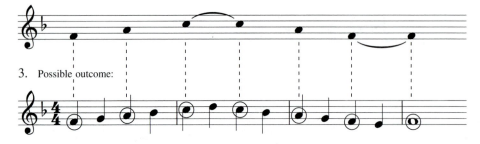

3. Possible outcome:

C Melodies (Major): M2 and m2

1. Establish the key for each of the following melodies by singing one of the *vocalises* presented earlier.
2. Using syllables or numbers, sing the melody.
3. Try to differentiate between neighboring and passing tone figures as you read each melody.

1. Scale: C Major

2. Scale: G Major

3. Scale: F Major

4. Scale: D Major

5. Scale: B-flat Major

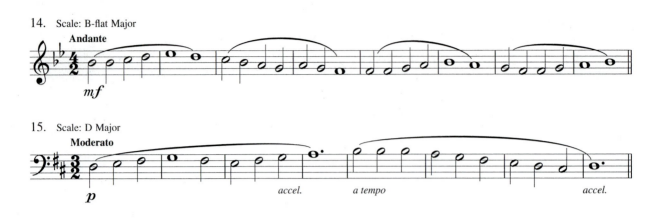

14. Scale: B-flat Major

15. Scale: D Major

The last four measures of number 16 are in contrary motion to the first four.

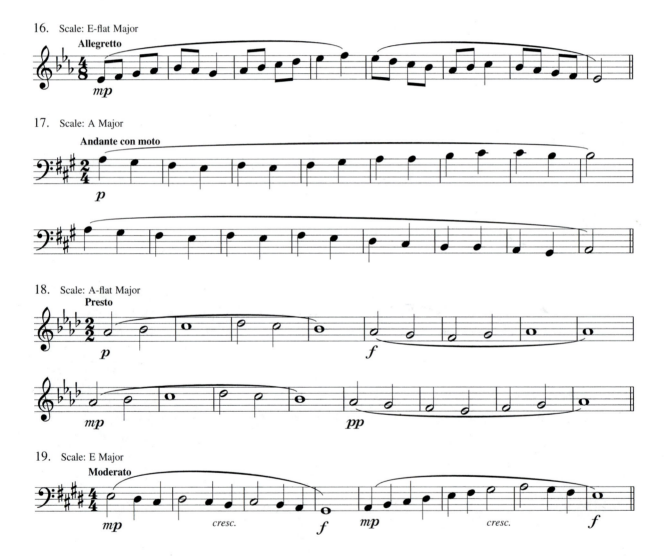

16. Scale: E-flat Major

17. Scale: A Major

18. Scale: A-flat Major

19. Scale: E Major

20. Scale: C Major

D Melodies (Major): P5, P4, M3, and m3 within the Tonic Triad and M2 and m2

1. Establish the key for each of the following melodies by singing a *vocalise*.
2. Using syllables or numbers, sing the melody.
3. Try to consider the elements of the triad as *reference tones*.

E ⬛ Ensembles—Two Voices: M2 and m2

SECTION 1. Ensemble Singing in Familiar Clefs

This two-voice section is intended to provide practice in ensemble singing in familiar clefs (treble and bass). The melody lines are similar to those found in part C of this unit, but now you must learn to think in two melodic dimensions. For individual practice, you could sing one line and play the other line at the keyboard. This would be excellent preparation for the classroom experience of singing in ensemble.

Follow the procedures outlined in part C for establishing the key.

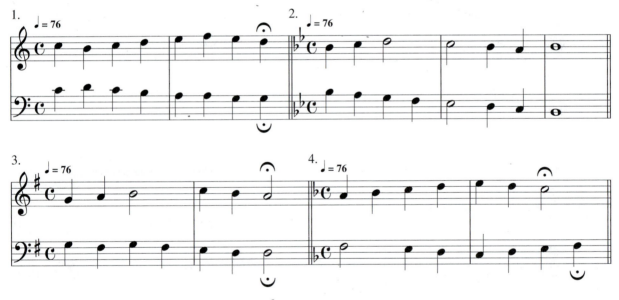

SECTION 2. Ensemble Singing in Unfamiliar Clefs

This two-voice section is intended to provide practice in ensemble singing in unfamiliar clefs (soprano, alto and tenor clefs). The placement of the clef on the staff indicates middle C. The soprano clef places middle C on the bottom line; the alto clef places middle C on the middle line; the tenor clef places middle C on the second line from the top.

The following excerpt will appear in all three clefs in this first unit to demonstrate how fluency in clef reading helps to build the skills required for the art of transposing from one key to another.

1. Both voices of the first excerpt are in the soprano clef. The starting note is G (key of C major).
2. Both voices of the second excerpt are in the alto clef. The starting note is C (key of F major).
3. Both voices of the third excerpt are in the tenor clef. The starting note is A (key of D major).

Johann Joseph Fux   #17 of Serie VII—Theoretische und pädigogische Werke from *Samtliche Werke* (Theoretical and Pedagogical Works, vol. VII of the Complete Works)

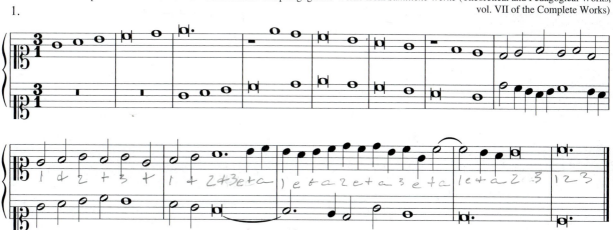

Reprinted by permission of Akademische Druck u. Verlagsanstalt, Graz, Austria.

Johann Joseph Fux   #17 of Serie VII—Theoretische und pädigogische Werke from *Samtliche Werke* (Theoretical and Pedagogical Works, vol. VII of the Complete Works)

2.

Reprinted by permission of Akademische Druck u. Verlagsanstalt, Graz, Austria.

Johann Joseph Fux   #17 of Serie VII—Theoretische und pädigogische Werke from *Samtliche Werke* (Theoretical and Pedagogical Works, vol. VII of the Complete Works)

3.

Reprinted by permission of Akademische Druck u. Verlagsanstalt, Graz, Austria.

UNIT TWO

A Rhythm—Compound Meter: Triple Division of the Beat

SECTION 1. Modules in Compound Meter

Using a neutral syllable, sing each of the given modules. Begin by repeating each module several times. Then treat the successive modules as a continuous exercise.

Notice that each beat in these modules is divisible by three. This triple division of the beat allows us to determine whether these modules are in compound meter as opposed to simple meter. Each beat in the compound meter of [$\frac{6}{8}$] is a dotted quarter note. Therefore, in [$\frac{6}{8}$] there are two beats, each divisible by three; in [$\frac{9}{8}$] three beats, each divisible by three; in [$\frac{12}{8}$] four beats, each divisible by three, and so on. Each beat in the compound meter of [$\frac{6}{4}$] is a dotted half note. Therefore, in [$\frac{6}{4}$] there are two beats, each divisible by three, and so on.

For a complete explanation of the division of the beat in compound meter, see Benward and Saker, *Music in Theory and Practice,* vol. 1 (7th ed.), pp. 10–11. An explanation of duple division of the beat in simple meter is given in unit 3.

Use the conducting pattern shown below if your instructor recommends you do so.

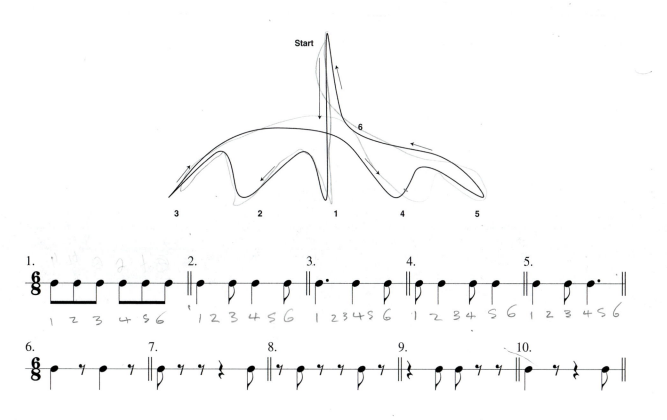

15

SECTION 2. Phrases in Compound Meter

For numbers 1–5, follow the procedures outlined in unit 1A, section 2. For the two-part exercises (6–9), the instructor should assign students to each part. Students should also be encouraged to practice these two-part exercises individually, using the left hand for tapping out the lower part and the right hand the upper part.

6. Rhythmic ostinato plus rhythmic imitation

7. Rhythmic alternation (examples also of rhythmic hocket)

8. Rhythmic imitation

9. Rhythmic imitation

SECTION 3. Creating a Coherent Phrase in Compound Meter

Return to section 1 and select four modules in the same meter. Place them in an order that creates a coherent four-measure phrase. Here is an example:

25.   24.   21.   22.

Write your solution on the following staff (or staves, in case you decide to write a two-voice composition):

Using a neutral syllable, sing your phrase and have your classmates identify which modules you selected and the order in which you sang them. At some future date, return to this phrase and add the melodic dimension. (If you have written a two-voice composition, perform one part on the piano while singing the other part with a neutral syllable.)

B Diatonic Models and Melodic Fragments for Interval Singing: P5, P4, M3, m3, M2, and m2

SECTION 1. Diatonic Models

These models anticipate the melodic fragments in the next section.

(A) INTERVALS OF THE 3rd OUTLINING P5s IN MAJOR KEYS

Use a G-major vocalise as a warm-up. Sing this exercise as written (in G major), and then transpose the entire set down a P5 to the key of C major. Continue the process through the keys of F, B♭, E♭, and so on.

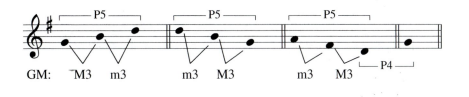

(B) PASSING TONE FIGURES IN MINOR FILLING IN 3rds

Follow the same procedure for passing tone figures in major keys. Use a vocalise in E minor (relative minor). For exercises in parallel minor, use a vocalise in G minor.

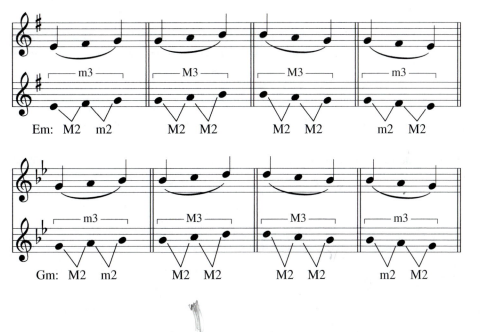

(C) INTERVALS OF THE P4, P5, AND M3 SUPPORTING A MELODIC ASCENT FROM $\hat{1}$–$\hat{3}$

Use a G major vocalise as a warm-up. After singing the intervals that outline scale degrees 1–3, sing the entire pattern in different keys as shown in the model:

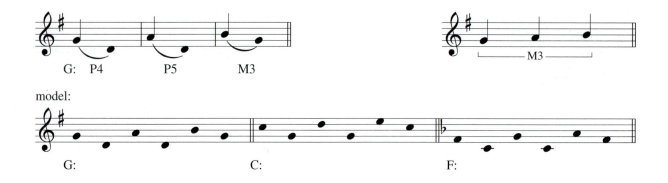

G: P4   P5   M3

M3

model:

G: C: F:

SECTION 2. Melodic Fragments in G Major (E Minor and G Minor)

These melodic fragments are taken from music literature for the purpose of providing a musical context for the intervals introduced in the previous section.

Follow the procedure outlined in unit 1B, section 2.

Bach   Chorale Cantata 26, *Ach wie nichtig, ach wie flüchtig* (Ah, How Empty! Ah, How Fleeting!) (transposed)

1a. Adagio

Em:

Bach   Chorale Cantata 26, *Ach wie nichtig, ach wie flüchtig* (Ah, How Empty! Ah, How Fleeting!) (transposed)

1b. Adagio

Gm:

Bach   Chorale, *Brunnquell aller Güter* (Fount [source] of All Goodness), BWV 445, meas. 1–6 (transposed)

2a. Adagio

Em:

Bach   Chorale, *Brunnquell aller Güter* (Fount [source] of All Goodness), BWV 445, meas. 1–6 (original key)

2b. Adagio

Gm:

Bach   Chorale, *Jesu, deine Liebeswunden* (Jesus, Your Wounds of Love), BWV 471, phrases 1 and 4 (transposed)

3a. Adagio

Em:

Bach   Chorale, *Jesu, deine Liebeswunden* (Jesus, Your Wounds of Love), BWV 471, phrases 1 and 4 (transposed)

3b. Adagio

Gm:

4.   Mozart   German Dance no. 5, K. 509 (transposed)

5.   Mozart   *Sanctus* from *Requiem*, K. 626, (transposed)

6.   Mozart   Eight Variations, K. 613, Variation 8 (transposed), meas. 1–4

7.   Mozart   Theme and Two Variations, K. 460 (454a) Theme (transposed and adapted), meas. 1–8

Mozart   "La belle Françoise" composed in Paris, 1778; the basis for Mozart's 12 Variations, K. 353 (300f), (transposed) meas. 1–4 (top line)

8.

Mozart   "La belle Françoise" composed in Paris, 1778; the basis for Mozart's 12 Variations, K. 353 (300f), (transposed) meas. 1–4 (middle line)

9.

Mozart   "La belle Françoise" composed in Paris, 1778; the basis for Mozart's 12 Variations, K. 353 (300f), (transposed) meas. 1–4 (bottom line)

10.

All three lines (8, 9, 10) should be combined in ensemble.

SECTION 3. Creating a Coherent Melody

Return to section 2 and select two or three segments of melodic fragments that create a coherent melody. It may be necessary to change the meter and rhythm of certain segments, depending on your choices. Here is an example based on measures 1 and 2 of fragment 1 and measures 2 and 3 of fragment 4.

SECTION 4. Improvisation

1.   Take melodic fragment 10* as the basis for improvising an upper voice.

*Mozart. "La belle Françoise" composed in Paris, 1778; the basis for Mozart's 12 Variations K. 353 (300 f), (transposed) meas. 1–4 (bottom line)

2.   Use the upper voice that you have created and improvise a new bass line. (For inspiration you might want to study the 12 Variations K. 353 (300 f) that Mozart composed on this tune.)

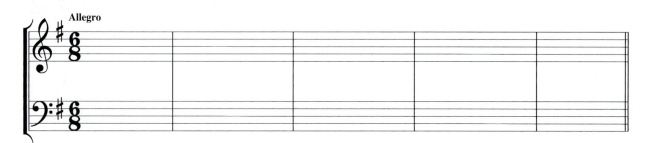

C Melodies (Major): P5, P4, M3, and m3 within the Tonic Triad and M2, and m2

The melodic content of this section focuses on some leaps within the tonic triad (M3, m3, P5, P4) as well as stepwise motion (M2 and m2) in C major.

These drills, although valuable for review and practice in singing at performance tempo, are suitable also for developing the art of clef reading as a means of transposing from one key to another. For example, the same phrase is used in both number 1 and number 11, except that in number 11 the alto clef is introduced. This places middle C (c') on the middle line. The alto clef in number 11 makes it possible to transpose number 1 to the key of D major without changing the position of any of the notes on the staff.

Procedure

1.   In your mind, replace the treble clef in number 2 with an alto clef (see number 11 to visualize an alto clef).
2.   Because all melodies in this section are in C major, you know that number 2 begins on the dominant (5, or Sol).

3. When you visualize number 2 with an alto clef, the first pitch is A (below middle C). A is now the dominant (5, or sol) and D is the tonic of the melody.

4. Imagine two sharps (F♯ and C♯) in the signature and sing the melody the same way as you sing it in C major with a treble clef.

5. If you sing the melody in the alto clef, it will be a 7th lower than in treble, but most melodies in this book are intended to be sung in whatever range the singer finds most comfortable.

6. If you have trouble reading in the alto clef, check your accuracy by going back to C major with a treble clef and singing the melody again.

7. Your unfamiliarity with this new clef will disappear presently, and you will have learned a valuable new skill that you may use many times later on.

D Melodies (Major): P5, P4, M3, and m3 within the Tonic Triad and M2 and m2

SECTION 1. Excerpts from Beethoven and Haydn

The following melodies excerpted from music literature illustrate the same intervals presented in part C of this unit.

Numbers 1–10 are from Beethoven's symphonic works, and 11–20 are from Haydn's keyboard compositions. For the purposes of this unit, some melodies have been slightly altered or abridged. The authors of this book adjusted the melodies to ensure a comfortable singing range and to stay within the rhythmic and melodic limitations imposed by the materials of the first two units. However, for those excerpts from Beethoven symphonies that were adapted, the original version is provided as well.

Sing these melodies using whatever procedures your instructor requests.

6.

Adapted from Beethoven   Symphony no. 7, op. 92, III

dolce
p

original

7.

Adapted from Beethoven   Symphony no. 7, op. 92, IV

Allegro con brio

ff

original

ff   *staccato*

8.

Adapted from Beethoven   Symphony no. 5, op. 67, IV

Allegro

ff

original

DRMFFMFSLASLTD

9.

Adapted from Beethoven   Symphony no. 8, op. 93, I

Allegro vivace e con brio

f

p   *dolce*

original

10.

Adapted from Beethoven   Symphony no. 9, op. 125 ("Freude")

Allegro assai

p

original

p

SECTION 2. Amish Songs and Hymn Tunes

The following are adapted Amish songs and hymn tunes.

"Jesus, Jesus, Source of Life"

1. ♩ = 88

"Jesus, Lover of My Soul"

2. ♩ = 112

"Come Ye Sinners"

3. ♩ = 88

"The Great Physician"

4. ♪ = 112

"Thousand Times by Me Be Greeted"

5. ♩ = 76

6.

"Author of the Whole Creation"

Fine

D.C. al Fine

7.

"When the Due Time Had Taken Place"

Fine

D.C. al Fine

8.

"Praise God Forever"

Fine

D.C. al Fine

E Ensembles—Two Voices: P5, P4, M3, and m3 within the Tonic Triad and M2 and m2

SECTION 1. Ensemble Singing in Familiar Clefs

The first three ensemble excerpts are from Beethoven's *Missa Solemnis,* op. 123: (1) Gloria, (2) Credo, and (3) Benedictus. Each melodic line operates within the same intervallic restrictions of this unit. The fourth excerpt, by Orlando di Lasso, provides another setting of the Benedictus written much earlier than the Beethoven.

Because each excerpt is imitative, sing each line as a separate melodic exercise before you try to put the two together. The texts from Gloria, Credo, and Benedictus are provided, although you need not use words in performing these.

1. Allegro vivace

Beethoven *Missa Solemnis,* op. 123, *Gloria* (adapted and transposed)

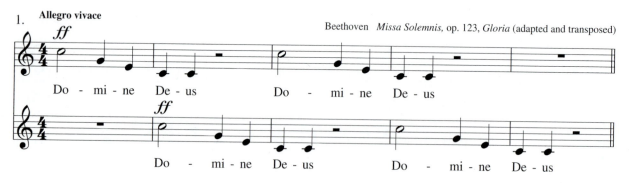

Do - mi - ne De - us   Do - mi - ne De - us

Do - mi - ne De - us   Do - mi - ne De - us

2.   Beethoven *Missa Solemnis,* op. 123, *Credo* (adapted and transposed)

Allegro molto

et   a -   scen   -   dit in coe - lum

Et   a -   scen   -   dit in coe   -   lum

3. **Andante molto cantabile e non troppo mosso**   Beethoven *Missa Solemnis,* op. 123, *Benedictus* (abridged)

Be - ne - di   -   ctus Qui__ ve - nit

Be - ne - di   -   ctus Qui__ ve - nit

in ___ no - mi - ne, no - mi - ne Do   -   mi - ni ___

in ___ no - mi - ne Do - mi - ni ___

* See section A of this unit for compound meter.
   As a warm-up for ensemble singing, each line should be performed as a solo exercise.
   When the students are ready to sing in ensemble, the instructor should provide the first few notes of each part at entrances, either by singing with the students or by articulating these patterns at the keyboard.

4.   Orlando di Lasso *Benedictus*

Cantus

Be   -   ne - di - ctus, _____ qui ve   -

Tenor

Be   -   ne - di - ctus, _____ qui

nit   in no - mi - ne _____ Do -

ve - nit   in no - mi - ne Do -

- mi - ni, in no - mi - ne, _____   in no - mi - ne, _____

- mi - ni,   in no - mi - ne, _____   in no - mi - ne, _____

_ in no - mi - ne _____ Do - mi - ni.

_ in no - mi - ne _____ Do - mi - ni.

New York: Appleton-Century-Crofts, Inc.—G. Soderlund

SECTION 2. Ensemble Singing in Unfamiliar Clefs

Johann Joseph Fux   #27 of Serie VII—Theoretische und pädigogische Werke from *Samtliche Werke* (Theoretical and Pedagogical Works, vol. VII of the Complete Works)

1.

Reprinted by permission of Akademische Druck u. Verlagsanstalt, Graz, Austria.

Johann Joseph Fux #28 of Serie VII—Theoretische und pädigogische Werke from *Samtliche Werke* (Theoretical and Pedagogical Works, vol. VII of the Complete Works)

2.

Reprinted by permission of Akademische Druck u. Verlagsanstalt, Graz, Austria.

UNIT THREE

A Rhythm—Simple Meter: Duple Division of the Beat

SECTION 1. Modules in Simple Meter

Using rhythm syllables or a neutral syllable, sing each of the given modules. Begin by repeating each module several times. Then treat the successive modules as a continuous exercise.

Notice that each beat in these modules is divisible by two. This duple division of the beat allows you to determine whether these modules are in simple meter or compound meter. Each beat in the simple meter of [$\frac{4}{4}$] is a quarter note. Therefore, in [$\frac{4}{4}$] there are four beats, each divisible by two; in [$\frac{3}{4}$] three beats, each divisible by two; and so on.

For a complete explanation of the division of the beat in simple meter, see Benward and Saker, *Music in Theory and Practice,* vol. 1 (7th ed.), p. 10.

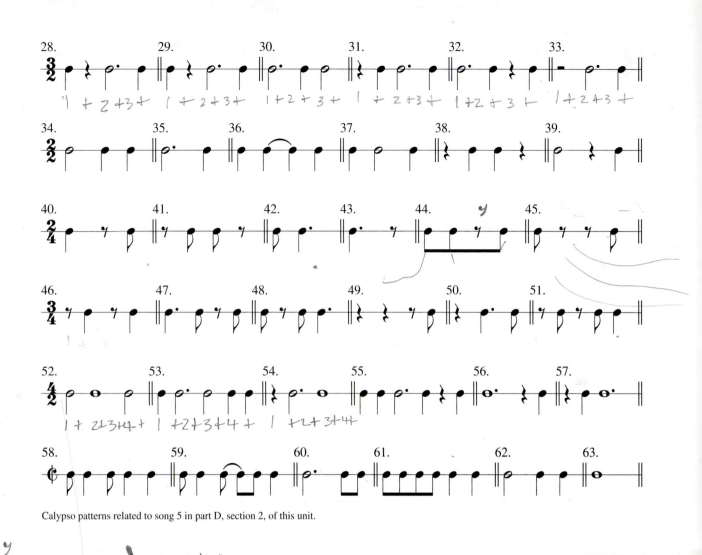

Calypso patterns related to song 5 in part D, section 2, of this unit.

SECTION 2. Phrases in Simple Meter with Duple Division of the Beat

For numbers 1–8, follow the procedures outlined in unit 1A, section 2. For the two-part exercises (9–10), follow the procedures outlined in unit 2A, section 2.

SECTION 3. Creating a Coherent Phrase in Simple Meter

Return to section 1 and select four modules in the same meter. Place them in an order that creates a coherent four-measure phrase. Here is an example:

Write your solution on the following line (or lines, in case you decided to write a two-voice composition):

Using a neutral syllable, sing your phrase and have your classmates identify which modules you selected and the order in which you sang them. At some future date, return to this phrase and add the melodic dimension. (If you have written a two-voice composition, perform one part on the piano while singing the other part with a neutral syllable.)

B   Diatonic Models and Melodic Fragments for Interval Singing: P8, P5, P4, M3, m3, M2, and m2

SECTION 1.   Diatonic Models

These models anticipate the melodic fragments in the next section.

(A) INTERVALS OUTLINING THE TONIC TRIAD AND DOMINANT 7th CHORD IN MAJOR

Use a D-major vocalise as a warm-up. For extra practice, sing these models in each of the major keys, moving down by fourths or up by fifths. See the following examples:

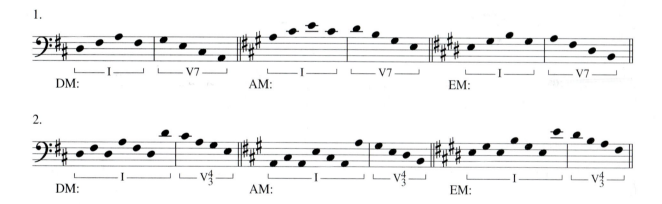

(B) INTERVALS EMPHASIZING THE TONIC TRIAD IN MINOR, WITH SPECIAL EMPHASIS ON THE PERFECT 4th

Use a B-minor vocalise as a warm-up. For extra practice, sing these models in each of the minor keys, moving down by 5ths or up by 4ths. Follow the same procedure for the D-minor excerpts. See the following examples:

SECTION 2. Melodic Fragments in D Major (B Minor and D Minor)

6. Menuetto

Mozart   Eight Minuets, K. 315g. I, meas. 1–4 (transposed)

7. Poco Andante

Beethoven   Piano Sonata op. 81a, II, meas. 176–177 (transposed)

8. Adagio

Mozart   Piano Sonata, K. 282 (189g), I, meas. 9–11 (rhythm reduced by half; transposed)

9. Allegro

Mozart   Twelve Variations, K. 179 (189a), Variation VIII, meas. 1–4 (transposed) (top line)

10. Allegro

Mozart   Twelve Variations, K. 179 (189a), Variation VIII, meas. 1–4 (transposed) (bottom line)

Both lines (9 and 10) should be combined in ensemble.

SECTION 3. Creating a Coherent Melody

Return to section 2 and select two or three segments of melodic fragments that create a coherent melody. It may be necessary to change the meter and rhythm of certain segments, depending on your choice. Here is an example based on measures 1 and 2 of fragment 3a and measures 3 and 4 of fragment 4a.

SECTION 4. Improvisation

1.   Take melodic fragment 10* as the basis for improvising an upper voice

* Mozart.   Twelve Variations, K 179 (189a), Variation VIII, meas. 1–4 (transposed) (bottom line)

2. Use the upper voice that you have created and improvise a new bass line. (For inspiration you might want to study each of Mozart's 12 Variations K 179 (189a)).

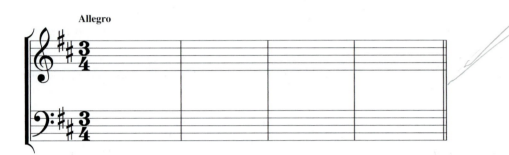

C Melodies (Major): P5, P4, M3, and m3 within the Tonic Triad and M2 and m2

Procedure for Completing Each Melody

1. Sing the scale on which the melody is constructed. Use syllables or numbers as suggested by your instructor.
2. When you are familiar with the scale, sing each melody using the same syllables or numbers.
3. Circle the 1st, 3rd, and 5th scale degrees as *reference tones* if you encounter difficulty.
4. Remember that you learn *only* when you sing the correct pitch and syllable or number. So, do not hesitate to repeat a melody until you are satisfied that you have sung it correctly.
5. Tempo is important. Sing each melody slowly at first. If you can increase the tempo without making mistakes, do so.

From *Games and Songs of American Children,* composed and compiled by William Wells Newell. Copyright, 1883, 1903, by Harper and Brothers, Copyright, 1911, by Robert B. Stone CURWEN & Sons London, Copyright 1914 by Grace Cleveland Porter

From *Games and Songs of American Children,* composed and compiled by William Wells Newell. Copyright, 1883, 1903, by Harper and Brothers, Copyright, 1911, by Robert B. Stone CURWEN & Sons London, Copyright 1914 by Grace Cleveland Porter

D Melodies (Minor)

SECTION 1. P5, P4, M3, and m3 within the Tonic Triad

1. Sing the scale related to each exercise—as usual, with syllables or numbers.
2. Sing each melody with the same syllables or numbers.
3. For the moment, do not worry about the intervals formed by scale steps 1, 3, and 5. Think of these primarily as *reference tones*—tones from which other scale degrees may be located.

SECTION 2. Natural, Harmonic, and Melodic Minor

The first example shows a single melody repeated to illustrate the three forms of the minor scale. Sing all three forms, one after the other, and note the effect created by each. Examples 2–4 are in natural minor. Example 5 combines features of natural minor and harmonic minor. For a complete explanation of natural, harmonic, and melodic minor, see Benward and Saker, *Music in Theory and Practice,* vol. 1 (7th ed.), pp. 29–32.

5. "The Land of the Humming Bird" (abridged)

SECTION 3. P5, P4, M3, and m3 within the Tonic Triad and M2 and m2

Follow procedures printed in part D, section 1, of this unit.

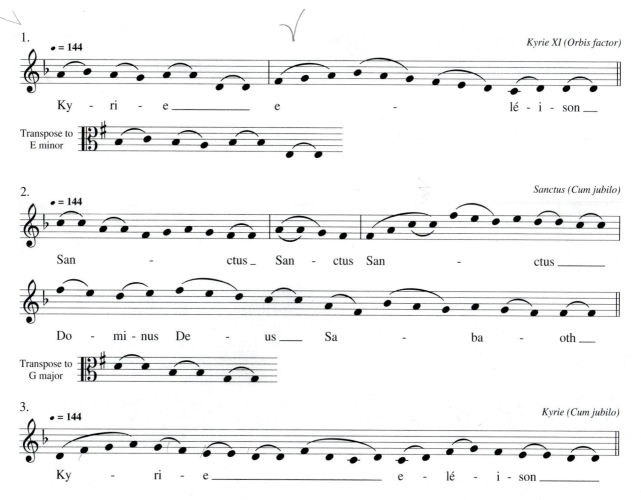

SECTION 4. Transposition and Inversion

For some additional practice in clef reading and transposition:

1. Transpose number 1 (*Kyrie XI—Orbis factor*). When you visualize the alto clef, think of the melody as being in E minor (Aeolian mode), so include F♯ in the signature.

2. Transpose number 2 (*Sanctus IX—Cum jubilo*). This was originally considered to be in the Ionian mode (now our major mode). When you visualize the alto clef, also add an F♯ to the key signature. The starting note is d'.

3. Melodies 3 and 4 are closely related. The *Kyrie IX* (Cum jubilo) (number 3) is the source for Josquin's *Missa de Beata Virgine* (number 4). The alto voice is shown here. When you visualize the alto clef, see whether you can figure out the correct signatures.

4. Melodies 5 and 6 are from Contrapunctus XII of Bach's *Art of Fugue;* number 6 is the melodic inversion of number 5.

4. **Lento**

Josquin des Prés *Kyrie eleison—Missa de Beata Virgine*

5.

Bach *Die Kunst der Fuge* (Art of Fugue), Contrapunctus 12 (Rectus)

6.

Bach *Die Kunst der Fuge* (Art of Fugue), Contrapunctus 12 (Inversus)

E Ensembles—Two Voices: P5, P4, M3, and m3 within the Tonic Triad and M2 and m2

SECTION 1. Ensemble Singing in Familiar Clefs

Follow the procedures given for unit 1E.

1.   2.

3.   4.

5.   6.

SECTION 2. Ensemble Singing in Unfamiliar Clefs

Orlando di Lasso *Cantiones duarum vocum* (Songs for Two Voices), from *Fantasia III*, meas. 1–11

Cantiones duarum vocum from *Fantasia III,* Dessoff Choir Series, edited by Paul Boepple © 1941. Used by permission of Carl Fischer for Mercury Music Corp.

UNIT FOUR

A Rhythm—Simple Meter: Quadruple Subdivision of the Beat

SECTION 1. Modules in Simple Meter

Using rhythm syllables or a neutral syllable, sing each of the given modules. Begin by repeating each module several times. Then treat the successive modules as a continuous exercise.

In these modules, you are subdividing the beat into four parts, representing the next logical ordering of the beat in the hierarchy of simple meter.

See unit 4C, exercise 1

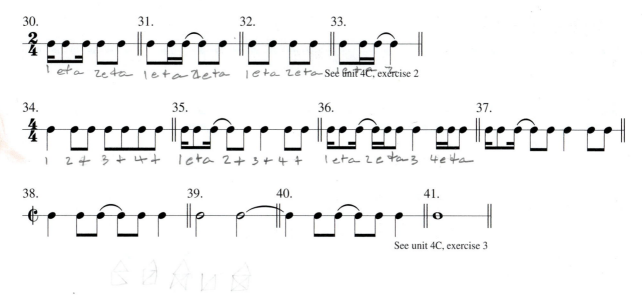

See unit 4C, exercise 2

See unit 4C, exercise 3

SECTION 2. Phrases in Simple Meter with Quadruple Division of the Beat

For numbers 1–5, follow the procedures outlined in unit 1A, section 2. For the two-part exercises (6–8), follow the procedures outlined in unit 2A, section 2.

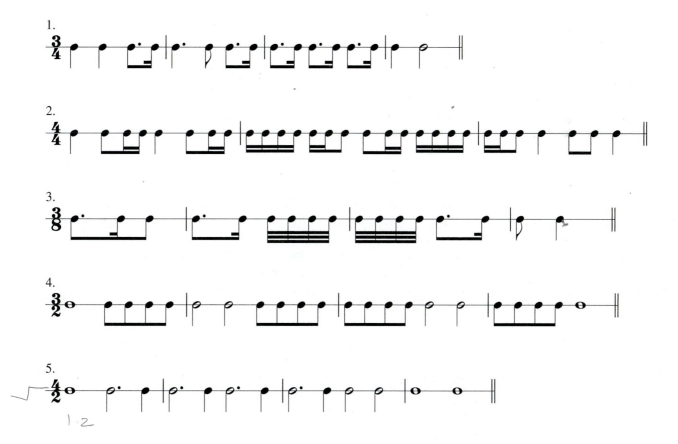

6. Rhythmic canon

7. Rhythmic canon

8. Rhythmic framework for Jamaican Folksong

See unit 4E1, exercise 9

SECTION 3. Creating a Coherent Phrase in Simple Meter

Return to section 1 and select four modules in the same meter. Place them in an order that creates a coherent four-measure phrase. Here is an example:

B Diatonic Models and Melodic Fragments for Interval Singing: m10, P8, P5, P4, M3, m3, M2, and m2

SECTION 1. Diatonic Models

These models anticipate the melodic fragments in the next section.

(A) INTERVALS OUTLINING THE TONIC TRIAD AND DOMINANT 7th CHORD

Use an A-major vocalise as a warm-up. For extra practice, sing this model in each of the major keys, using the last note of the pattern as the first note of the same pattern transposed a 4th lower or a 5th higher. See the following model:

(B) INTERVALS EMPHASIZING THE INTERVALS P4 AND P5, FILLING IN AN OCTAVE

For extra practice, this model can be repeated in all the minor keys by singing the pattern down a P5 (or up a P4) through all 12 keys. See the following model:

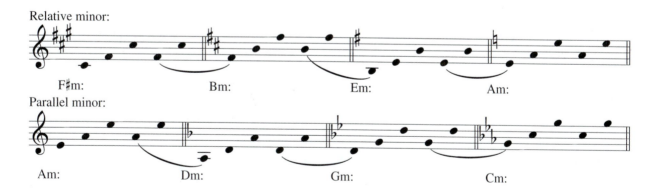

(C) INTERVALS OF THE P5, P4, M3, AND m3, FILLING IN AN OCTAVE

For extra practice, this model may be repeated in all minor keys by singing the pattern down a P5 (up a P4).

Relative minor:

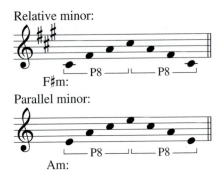

F♯m:

Parallel minor:

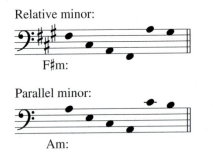

Am:

(D) INTERVALS OF THE m10, P4, M3, AND m3 OUTLINING THE TONIC TRIAD

This model provides an unusual example of a tonic triad because the interval of a m10 occurs between the root and the 3rd. For extra practice, repeat this pattern in all minor keys.

Relative minor:

F♯m:

Parallel minor:

Am:

SECTION 2. Melodic Fragments in A Major (F♯ Minor and A Minor)

1.
Allegro
Mozart *Eine kleine Nachtmusik* (A Little Night Music), K. 525 (transposed)

2a.
Allegro con brio
Wagner *Die fliegende Holländer* (The Flying Dutchman), Overture (first theme transposed)

3a.
Allegro
Schubert Symphony no. 5, Minuet (transposed)

4a. **Allegro assai**
Mozart *Idomeneo*, act I, Aria (Electra) (transposed)
fp

5a. Andante molto moderato ♩ = 84   Gabriel Fauré *Pavane,* op. 50, meas. 1–5 (original key) (top line)

6a. Andante molto moderato ♩ = 84   Gabriel Fauré *Pavane,* op. 50, meas. 1–5 (original key) (middle line)

7a. Andante molto moderato ♩ = 84   Gabriel Fauré *Pavane,* op. 50, meas. 1–5 (original key) (bottom line)

All three lines (5, 6, 7) should be combined in ensemble.

2b. Allegro con brio   Wagner *Die fliegende Holländer,* Overture (first theme transposed)

3b. Allegro   Schubert Symphony no. 5, Minuet (transposed)

4b. Allegro assai   Mozart *Idomeneo,* act I, Aria (Electra) (transposed)

5b. Andante molto moderato ♩ = 84   Gabriel Fauré *Pavane,* op. 50, meas. 1–5 (transposed) (top line)

6b. Andante molto moderato ♩ = 84   Gabriel Fauré *Pavane,* op. 50, meas. 1–5 (transposed) (middle line)

7b. Andante molto moderato ♩ = 84   Gabriel Fauré *Pavane,* op. 50, meas. 1–5 (transposed) (bottom line)

All three lines (5, 6, 7) should be combined in ensemble.

8. **Andantino**   Mozart *Die Zauberflöte* (The Magic Flute), Duet Pamina, Papageno, meas. 7–9 (transposed) (top line)

9. **Andantino**   Mozart *Die Zauberflöte* (The Magic Flute), Duet Pamina, Papageno, meas. 23–25 (transposed) (top line)

10. **Andantino**   Mozart *Die Zauberflöte* (The Magic Flute), Duet Pamina, Papageno, meas. 7–9 (transposed) (bottom line)

Two lines can be combined in ensemble (8 and 10; 9 and 10)

SECTION 3.   Creating a Coherent Melody

Return to section 2 and select two or three segments of melodic fragments that create a coherent melody. It may be necessary to change the meter and rhythm of certain segments, depending on your choice. Here is an example based on measures 1 and 2 of fragment 2a, measures 2 and 3 of fragment 3a, and measure 4 of fragment 2a.

SECTION 4.   Improvisation

1.   Take melodic fragment 7a as the basis for improvising an upper voice
     Gabriel Fauré *Pavane,* op. 50, meas. 1–5 (original key) (bottom line)

2. Use the upper voice that you have created and improvise a new bass line. (For inspiration you might want to study the musical score for Gabriel Fauré's *Pavane,* op. 50.)

3. Take melodic fragment 10 as the basis for improvising an upper voice
   Mozart *Die Zauberflöte* (The Magic Flute), Duet Pamina, Papageno, meas. 7–9 (transposed) (bottom line)

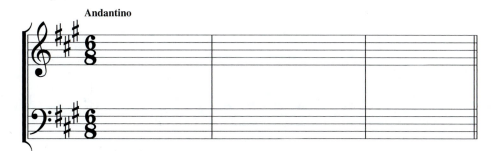

4. Use the upper voice that you have created and improvise a new bass line. (For inspiration you might want to study the musical score for The Magic Flute.)

C Melodies (Major and Minor): P5, P4, M3, m3, M2, and m2

These melodies are limited to the same skips as those in unit 3C except that the skips may occur between scale degrees other than 1-3-5.

Melodies 1–3 are in major and include calypso rhythm patterns, introduced in part A of this unit (modules 26–41). All other melodies are in minor and utilize rhythm patterns introduced in previous units.

Melodies 4–12 are in minor and are taken from a publication entitled *Selected Jewish Songs* (for members of the armed forces, published by the National Jewish Welfare Board in cooperation with American Association for Jewish Education, copyright 1942, Jewish Welfare Board, member agency USO).

Follow the directions as outlined in unit 3C.

See unit 4A, exercises 26–29

See unit 4A, exercises 30–33, and unit 5B, section 2, exercise 8.

"Ratta Madan Law" and "Mattie Rag" from *Jamaica, Land We Love,* compiled by Lloyd Hall.

See unit 4A, exercises 38–41

BACK TO THE TROPICS Words and music by Lionel Belasco and Leighla Whipper. © EMI Mills Music, Inc. Worldwide print rights administered by Alfred Publishing Co., Inc. All rights reserved.

12.   "Hasivenu Elecha" (Bring Us Back to You)

With abandon

D Melodies (Major and Minor): P5, P4, M3, m3, M2, and m2

These melodies are limited to the same skips as those of unit 3C, except that the skips may occur between scale degrees other than 1-3-5.

SECTION 1. Schubert Songs

All melodies in this section are excerpted from the songs of Franz Schubert. Nearly all the rhythm patterns in these songs were already presented, except for the simple triplet in numbers 6 and 9; the three notes of the triplet should be spaced evenly over one complete beat.

1. **Ziemlich schnell**

Schubert *Estarrung* (Chill) from *Winterreise*, op. 89, no. 4 , D. 911

2. **Mässig**

Schubert *Am Flusse* (On the River), D. 766

3. **Mässig**

Schubert *Schweizerlied* (Swiss Song), D. 559

4. **Nicht zu geschwind, doch kräftig**

Schubert *Aufenthalt* (Abode) from *Schwanengesang*, no. 5, D. 318

5.   Etwas langsam   Schubert *Der Leiermann* (The Organ Grinder) fro...

6.   Mässig   Schubert *Der Lindenbaum* (The Linden Tree) from *Winterreise,* op. 89, no. 5, D. 911

7.   Etwas geschwind ♩. = 76   Schubert *Drang in die Ferne* (Urge to Roam), D. 770

8.   Ziemlich lebhaft   Schubert *Der Musensohn* (The Son of the Muses), D. 764a

9.   Mässige Bewegung   Schubert *Zwei Szenen aus "Lacrimas"* II (Delphine), op. 124, no. 1, D. 857 (2)

2. Clef Reading

on contains excerpts from the first movement of Schubert's "Unfinished" Symphony.

Procedures

1. Example 1 consists of the opening melody (mm. 13–20), played in unison by two oboes and two clarinets in A. To sing the clarinet part as it sounds, try to think in the soprano clef, with c' (middle C) on the bottom line. Experiment by using letter names and by checking your accuracy with the oboe part. Remember that the oboe is a nontransposing instrument and sounds the same pitches as the clarinet in A.

2. Example 2, from the same movement (mm. 291–298), also features different instruments playing melodies at the same pitch: violas (Vla) and cellos (Vc). Because these instruments are nontransposing, it is not necessary for you to use clefs for the purpose of changing key. Cello parts are sometimes written in the tenor clef but most often in the bass clef.

3. In this excerpt, the same melodic figure appears four times. For the purposes of this exercise, it is advised to consider the following temporary tonic pitches:

> mm. 291–292—F♯ minor
> mm. 293–294—E major
> mm. 295–296—C♯ minor
> mm. 297–298—B major

1.   Schubert Symphony no. 8 ("Unfinished"), D. 759, B Minor, I (mm. 13–20)

2.   Schubert Symphony no. 8 ("Unfinished"), D. 759, B Minor, I (mm. 291–298)

E Ensembles

SECTION 1. Ensemble Singing in Familiar Clefs

The first eight excerpts are from chorale melodies harmonized by Bach. The ninth excerpt represents the outer voices of a Jamaican folk song. The rhythmic framework for this excerpt was presented in part A, section 2, number 8 of this unit. A tempo of ♩ = 72–80 is suggested for all examples.

Follow the procedures outlined in unit 1E, for ensemble singing.

1. Chorale *Meinen Jesum laß' ich nicht, weil* (I Will Not Leave My Jesus), BWV 380

2. Chorale *Für Freuden laßt uns springen* (Let Us Leap with Joy), BWV 313

3. Chorale *Ihr Gestirn', ihr hohlen Lüfte* (Ye Stars, Ye Airy Winds), BWV 476

4. Chorale *Herr Gott, dich loben alle wir* (Lord God, We All Praise Thee), BWV 328

5. Chorale *Christe, der du bist Tag und Licht* (Christ, Who Art Day and Light), BWV 274

6. Chorale *Singt dem Herrn ein neues Lied* (Sing the Lord a New Song), BWV 411

7. Cantata 42 *Verleih' uns Frieden gnädiglich* (Mercifully Grant Us Peace)

8. Chorale *Christus, der uns selig macht* (Christ, Who Makes Us Blessed), BWV 283

9. **With disdain**

bass line adapted

See unit 4A, section 2, exercise 8

"Big, Big Sambo Gal" from *Jamaica, Land We Love,* compiled by Lloyd Hall.

SECTION 2. Ensemble Singing in Unfamiliar Clefs

For the following example from Haydn's String Quartet op. 17, no. 5, Minuet and Trio, students are invited to bring their instruments to class.

Haydn String Quartet op. 17, no. 5, II

Menuetto

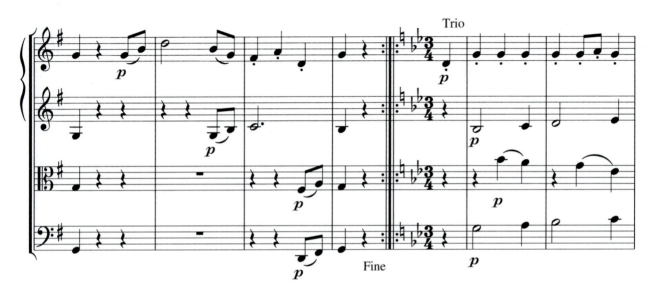

Attacca subito il Menuetto

UNIT FIVE

A Rhythm—Simple Meter: Irregular Division of the Beat (the Triplet)

SECTION 1. Modules in Simple Meter

Using rhythm syllables or a neutral syllable, sing each of the given modules. Begin by repeating each module several times. Then treat the successive modules as a continuous exercise.

In these modules, we are introducing the triplet, which represents an irregular division of the beat in simple meter. For a useful example that shows the differences between regular and irregular divisions of the beat, see Benward and Saker, *Music in Theory and Practice,* vol. 1 (7th ed.), figure 1.39, p. 16.

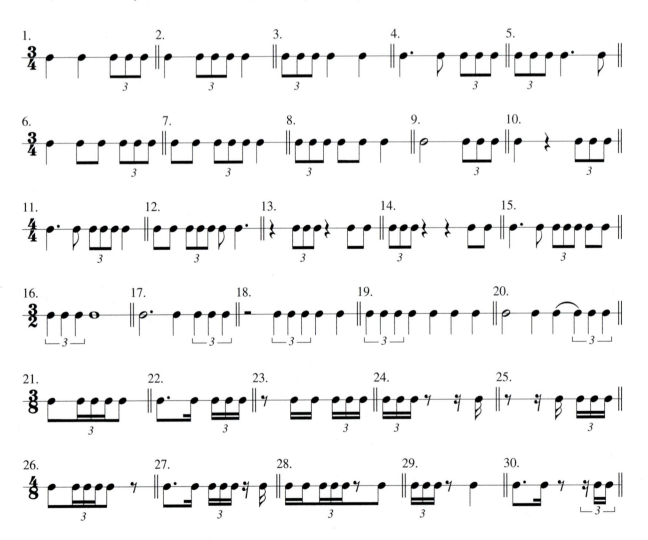

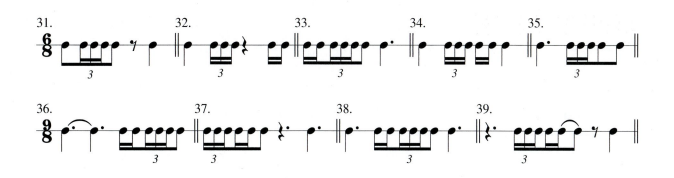

SECTION 2. Phrases in Simple Meter with Irregular Division of the Beat (the Triplet)

For numbers 1–5, follow the procedures outlined in unit 1A, section 2. For the two-part exercises (6–7), follow the procedures outlined in unit 2A, section 2.

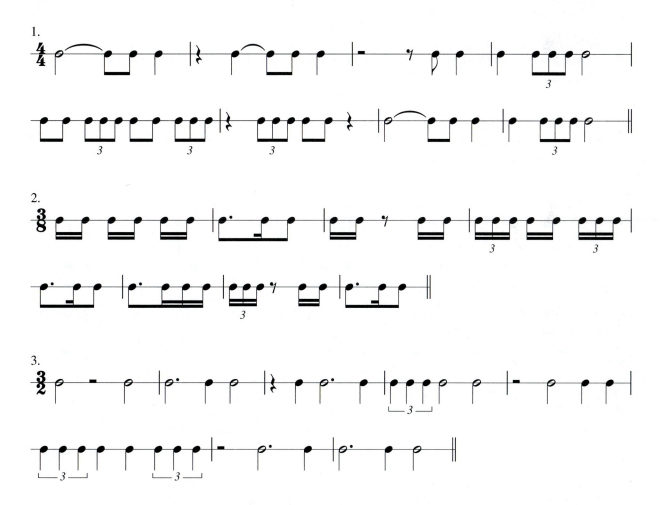

SECTION 3. Creating a Coherent Phrase in Simple Meter with a Triplet as an Example of an Irregular Division of the Beat

Return to section 1 and select three or four rhythm modules. Place them in an order that creates a coherent four-measure phrase. Because this procedure is clear, no example is provided here.

Write your solution on the following line:

B Diatonic Models and Melodic Fragments for Interval Singing—New Intervals: M6 and m6

SECTION 1. Diatonic Models

These models anticipate the melodic fragments in the next section.

These exercises emphasize intervals of the major 6th (M6) from scale degree 5 (C) in an ascending motion to scale degree 3 (A) before moving in a descending motion to scale degree 1 (F). Follow the same procedure as in previous units. For extra practice, sing these exercises in all major keys, transposing to each new key by P5s down or P4s up.

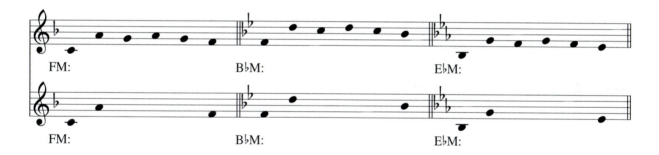

FM: BbM: EbM:

FM: BbM: EbM:

This model opens with the ascending M6 from scale degree 5 (C) up to scale degree 3 (A) and continues in an ascending motion to scale degree 1 (F).

FM:

Here the minor 6th (m6) is a chordal skip. The m6 (F down to A) functions as a consonant skip in support of the final pitch, C.

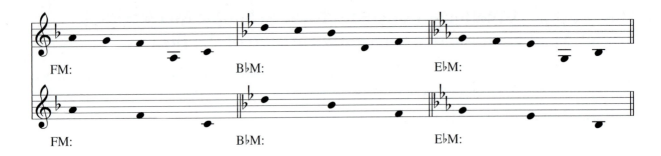

In this set, the major 6th (M6) is part of III in pure (natural) minor.

The sequential relationship of these exercises (F major) with triads on F and D is similar to that of the previous example, except that the tonic of the previous exercise is D minor. Use the same procedures as earlier.

These exercises outline the D-minor tonic triad. In this section, which serves as preparation for the singing of the melodic fragments, the authors recommend drills in relative minor rather than parallel minor because of the tonal design of melodic fragments 4 and 5, which begin in F major and end in D minor.

This exercise introduces the M6 as a descending pattern from scale degree 3 (A) to scale degree 5 (C), first as part of a triadic pattern and then in combination with a m6 from scale degree 6 (D) to scale degree 4 (Bb).

SECTION 2. Melodic Fragments in F Major (and D minor)

1. Andante ♪ = 132
Chopin   Nocturne op. 9, no. 2 (transposed)

2. Lento
Chopin   Nocturne op. 62, no. 2 (transposed)

3. Lento sostenuto ♩. = 50
Chopin   Nocturne op. 27, no. 2 (transposed)

4. Lento ♩. = 60
Chopin   Nocturne op. 15, no. 3 (transposed)

5. Lento sostenuto
Chopin   Nocturne op. 55, no. 2 (transposed)

6. Allegro molto agitato ♩. = 96
Chopin   Etude op. 10, no. 9 (transposed)

7. In a carefree style
Jamaica   "Mattie walla lef"

From *Jamaica, Land We Love,* compiled by Lloyd Hall.

8. Not too fast
Jamaica   "Mattie Rag" (transposed)

See unit 4C, exercise 2.

From *Jamaica, Land We Love,* compiled by Lloyd Hall.

9. **Slowish** ♩ = 54   Grainger *Colonial Song*

10. **Flowingly** ♩ = 80–88   Grainger *Irish Tune from County Derry*

Irish Tune from County Derry. Copyright 1930 by Percy Grainger, International Copyright secured. Printed in the USA. G. Schirmer, Inc.

SECTION 3. Creating a Coherent Melody

Return to section 2 and select two or three segments of melodic fragments that create a coherent melody. It may be necessary to change the meter and rhythm of certain segments, depending on your choice.

SECTION 4. Improvisation

1. The following accompaniment figure is adapted from Chopin's Nocturne opus 27, no. 2 (transposed). Recall that melodic fragment 3 is from the same piece. Use the accompaniment figure as the basis for improvising an upper voice.

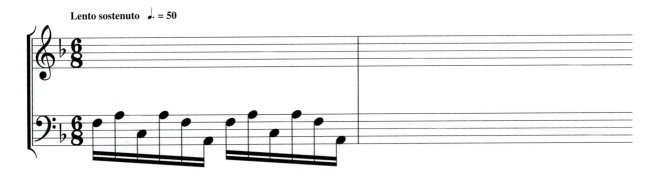

Lento sostenuto ♩. = 50

2. Use the upper voice that you have created and improvise a new bass line. (For inspiration, you might want to study the musical score for several of Chopin's Nocturnes.)

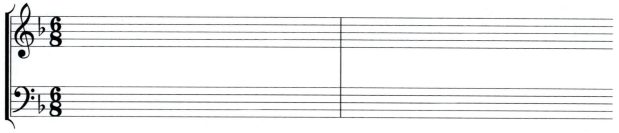

3. The following accompaniment figure is adapted from Chopin's Nocturne opus 9, no. 2 (transposed). Recall that melodic fragment 1 is from the same piece. Use the accompaniment figure as the basis for improvising an upper voice.

4. Use the upper voice that you have created and improvise a new bass line. (For inspiration, you might want to study the musical score for several of Chopin's Nocturnes.)

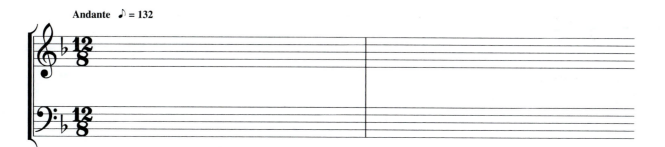

C Melodies (Major and Minor)—New Intervals: M6 and m6

The next six songs are from a collection titled *Six Creole Folk-Songs* (music arranged and translations by Maud Cuney Hare). Some of the rhythmic and melodic fragments found in these songs emphasize the models of parts A and B of this unit.

1. **Allegretto** ♩ = 84

2. **Animato** ♩ = 88

3. **Allegretto** ♩ = 72   ♩ = 88

"Quand mo-té jeune" (Bal fini) (Dance song)

4. **Con moto** ♩ = 116

"Aine, dé, trois, Caroline" (Song of Longing)

5. **Allegro** ♩ = 92

6. **Lentement** ♩ = 80

Exercises 1–6 from *Six Creole Folk-Songs.* Music arranged and translations by Maud Cuney Hare © by Carl Fischer, New York, 1921.

D Melodies (Major and Minor)—New Intervals: M6 and m6

The format of this section resembles that of part B ("Diatonic Models and Melodic Fragments for Interval Singing") in that selected melodies are written in or transposed to the same key. Here, the melodies are in either G major or E minor. Because of the nature of these songs, it is an advantage to study them within the framework of the same key signature. For example, the key signature of E minor helps clarify the similarity between melodic patterns in two selections that are in natural minor: number 2, "Monday, Tuesday," from Ireland, and number 3, "The Laughter of Raindrops," from Jamaica. The modal flavor of the subtonic triad (D, F♯, A) in relation to the tonic triad (E, G, B) provides the link of continuity between these songs. In this section, some of the major melodies tilt toward relative minor and some of the minor melodies toward relative major.

1.   Joe Primrose   "St. James Infirmary" (abridged)

Moderato

Mournfully

2. **Larghetto** ♩. = 60 — Traditional "Da Luain, da Mairt" (Monday, Tuesday) Southern Counties, Ireland (transposed)

3. Kathleen McFarlane (Jamaica) "The Laughter of Raindrops" (abridged)

"The Laughter of Raindrops" Music by Kathleen McFarlane, Words by Lisa Salmon. From *Jamaica, Land We Love,* compiled by Lloyd Hall.

Andrea Gabrieli (uncle of Giovanni Gabrieli) "A caso un giorno" (One Day by Chance), from *First Book of Madrigals* for three voices
(transposed)*

4. ♩ = 60

*Melody only; three-voice madrigal is given in the next section in the original key.

Adapted from "A caso un giorno," by Andrea Gabrieli and published in *Andrea Gabrieli: Complete Madrigals 1:* Madrigals of Libro primo a 3; Canzone of Petrarch a 3; Giustiniane a 3; edited by Tillman Merritt. Recent Researches in the Music of the Renaissance, vol. 41. Madison, Wisconsin: A-R Editions, Inc. 1981. Used with permission.

5.   Kathleen McFarlane (Jamaica)   "Henry Morgan" (abridged) (transposed)

Bold with well defined rhythm

"Henry Morgan" music by Kathleen McFarlane, from *Jamaica, Land We Love,* compiled by Lloyd Hall.

6.   Ireland "A New Song Called Granuaile"

7. **Andante**   "I Will Walk with My Love" (a fragment) County Dublin, Ireland (transposed)

8.   Ireland "The Piper's Tunes"

Chorus

Ri - too - ral - oo - ral - ah,   Ri - too - ral - oo - ral - ad - dy,   Ri - too - ral - oo - ral - ah   Ri - too - ral - oo - ral - ad - dy.

9.   Jamaican Folk Song   "Cookie"

Questioningly

From *Jamaica, Land We Love,* compiled by Lloyd Hall.

10.   Jamaican Folk Song   "Wata come a me eye" (transposed)

Tenderly

From *Jamaica, Land We Love,* compiled by Lloyd Hall.

11.   Ireland   "Lillibulero" (transposed)

Chorus

Lè - ro lè - ro lè - ro lè - ro Lil - li - bu - lè - ro bul - len a la

Lil - li bu - lè - ro lè - ro lè - ro Lil - li bu - lè ro bul - len a la

Jamaican Folk Song "Cudelia Brown" (transposed)

12. **Amusingly**

From *Jamaica, Land We Love*, compiled by Lloyd Hall.

E Ensembles

SECTION 1. Ensemble Singing in Familiar Clefs

Andrea Gabrieli (uncle of Giovanni Gabrieli) "A caso un giorno" (One Day by Chance), from *First Book of Madrigals* for three voices

1. Tansillo

Prima Stanza

♩ = 60

Canto 2

A ca-so un gior - no mi gui-dò la sor - te,

Canto

A ca-so un gior - no mi gui-dò la sor - te, mi gui-dò la sor - te

Basso

A ca-so un gior - no

Adapted from "A caso un giorno," by Andrea Gabrieli, and published in *Andrea Gabrieli: Complete Madrigals 1:* Madrigals of Libro primo a 3; Canzone of Petrarch a 3; Giustiniane a 3; edited by Tillman Merritt. Recent Researches in the Music of the Renaissance, vol. 41. Madison, Wisconsin: A-R Editions, Inc. 1981. Used with permission.

2.

Andrea Gabrieli   "Che giova posseder" (What Good Does It Do to Possess Cities and Kingdoms)

Adapted from "Che giova posseder," by Andrea Gabrieli, and published in *Andrea Gabrieli: Complete Madrigals 1:* Madrigals of Libro primo a 3; Canzone of Petrarch a 3; Giustiniane a 3; edited by Tillman Merritt. Recent Researches in the Music of the Renaissance, vol. 41. Madison, Wisconsin: A-R Editions, Inc. 1981. Used with permission.

SECTION 2. Ensemble Singing in Unfamiliar Clefs

In the following Ballade no. 11 "N'en fait n'en dit, n'en pensee" (Nothing Done, Nothing Said, Nothing Thought) written by Guillaume de Machaut in the fourteenth century, the lower voice was intended to be performed by an instrument to accompany the upper line. Students should be reminded to bring their instruments to class to provide accompaniment to the vocal line.

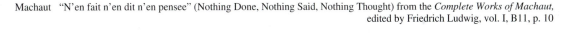

Machaut   "N'en fait n'en dit n'en pensee" (Nothing Done, Nothing Said, Nothing Thought) from the *Complete Works of Machaut,* edited by Friedrich Ludwig, vol. I, B11, p. 10

eins yert de cuer vray de moy

ser - vie et a - me - e,

tant com je vi - vray.

Printed with the friendly permission of Breitkopf & Härtel, Wiesbaden.

UNIT SIX

A Rhythm—Simple Meter: More Difficult Quadruple Subdivision of the Beat

SECTION 1. Modules in Simple Meter

Using rhythm syllables or a neutral syllable, sing each of the given modules. Begin by repeating each module several times. Then treat the successive modules as a continuous exercise.

Just as in the modules of unit 4, we are subdividing the beat into four parts.

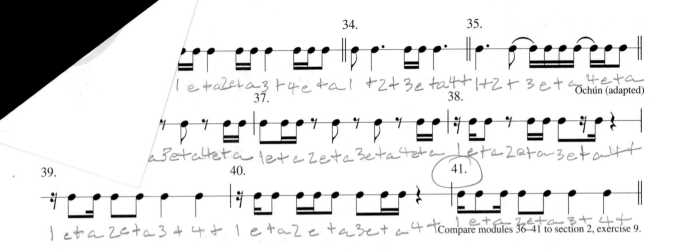

Ochún (adapted)

Compare modules 36–41 to section 2, exercise 9.

SECTION 2. Phrases in Simple Meter

2. Rhythmic crescendo and decrescendo

5.

6. Alternating $\frac{2}{4}$ and $\frac{3}{4}$; see "The Raftsmen's Song," in this unit

7. The upper voice is a rhythmic augmentation of the first four bars of the lower voice.

8. Rhythmic ostinato

Adapted from *The Music of Santería,* pp. 109–110. *Traditional Rhythms of the Batá Drums,* by John Amira and Steven Cornelius (Crown Point, Ind. White Cliffs Media Company, 1992). "This book presents the salute (or praise) rhythms of batá drumming. The most sacred and complex of the ritual music associated with the Afro-Cuban religion Santería" (p. 1). "Batá are double-headed, hourglass shaped drums" (p. 15). "Ochún—a river deity, Ochún is the goddess of love and beauty" (p. 109).

9. Ochún

SECTION 3. Creating a Coherent Phrase in Simple Meter

Return to section 1 and select three or four rhythm modules. Place them in an order that creates a coherent four-measure phrase.

Write your solution on the following line:

B Diatonic Models and Melodic Fragments for Interval Singing—Review: M6 and m6

SECTION 1. Diatonic Models

These models anticipate the melodic fragments in the next section.

These exercises emphasize intervals of the chordal skips within a major tonic triad starting with the root, moving down to the 5th and then up to the 3rd. The upward skip from scale degree 5 to scale degree 3 results in the interval of a major 6th (M6). Follow the same procedure as in previous units. For extra practice, sing these exercises in all major keys, transposing to each new key by P5s down or P4s up. The tossing of triads among students should continue, as shown in the following model:

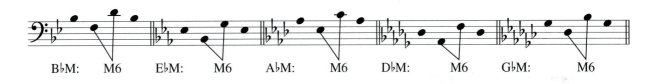

The first three melodic fragments (Mozart, Beethoven, and Makeba) follow a similar melodic contour.

These exercises emphasize the chordal skips within a major tonic triad, starting with the root, moving to the 3rd, and then down to the 5th. The downward skip from scale degree 3 to scale degree 5 results in a major 6th (M6). Follow the same procedures as in previous units. Sing the model in all major keys, transposing in the manner described in each previous unit.

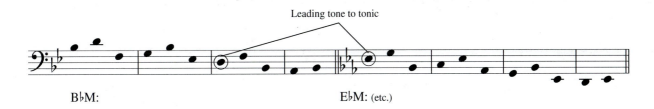

The tonic and subdominant triads are outlined. The dominant is implied only with the leading tone as it progresses to tonic.

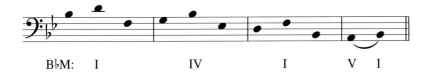

These exercises combine the major and minor 6th patterns that form the basis of melodic fragments 5, 6, and 7. Follow the same procedure as described in previous units, using the following model as the basis for transposition.

This model emphasizes the ascending major 6th (M6), followed by a descending scale line, and may be thought of in Bb major as well as G minor. This exercise is related to fragments 8–10.

SECTION 2. Melodic Fragments in B♭ Major (B♭ Minor and G Minor)

1.
Mozart   *Requiem*, K. 626, *Tuba Mirum*
Andante

2.
Beethoven   *Fidelio* (Overture), op. 72C (transposed and adapted)
Allegro

3.
African Folk Song   Makeba   "Dubula" (Shoot) (transposed)
♩ = 160

4.
Mozart   Minuet, K. 2, no. 2 (transposed)
Allegro

5.
Mussorgsky   *Boris Godounov* (Opera), scene 2 (transposed)
Moderato

6a.
Mozart   *Requiem*, K. 626, *Lacrymosa* (Tears)
Larghetto

6b.
Mozart   *Requiem*, K. 626, *Lacrymosa* (Tears) (transposed)
Larghetto

7a. Schubert Variation on a Waltz by Diabelli, D. 718

Andante

7b. Schubert Variation on a Waltz by Diabelli, D. 718 (transposed)

Andante

8. Tchaikovsky Symphony no. 5, op. 64 (transposed)

Andante ♩ = 80

p   *più* *f*   *mf*

9. Mozart Six German Dances, no. v, K. 509 (transposed)

Allegro

10. Mahler *Wer hat dies Liedlein erdacht* (Up There on the Hill) from *Des Knaben Wunderhorn* (The Youth's Magic Horn) (transposed)

With easy gaiety

SECTION 3. Creating a Coherent Melody

Return to section 2 and select two or three segments of melodic fragments that create a coherent melody. It may be necessary to change the meter and rhythm of certain segments, depending on your choice.

SECTION 4. Improvisation

The following bass line is taken from the Tenor *David* used by Machaut as the basis for a "double hocket." Twenty-two measures are provided in this excerpt. Notice that the rhythmic *talea* extends from measures 1–11 and that the same succession of rhythmic values recurs in measures 12–22. All three voices of measures 1–22 appear in part E, section 2 of this unit. Before looking at Machaut's complete realization of this excerpt, use this "isorhythmic bass" line as a basis for creating one upper voice. Then create a new isorhythmic bass to accompany the newly created upper voice.

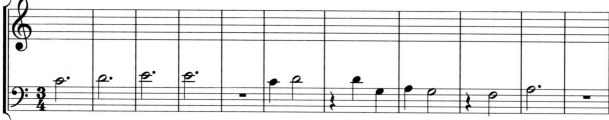

Printed with the friendly permission of Breitkopf & Härtel, Wiesbaden.

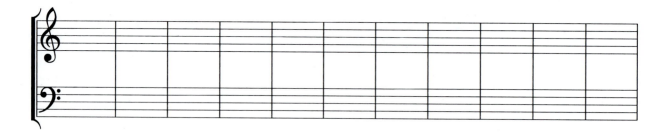

C Melodies (Major and Minor): M6 and m6

Songs 1–4 in this section include folk songs from the northern woods of the United States and the cities of Basel and Lausanne, Switzerland. Some of the rhythm and melodic fragments found in these songs emphasize the models of parts A and B of this unit.

1.   "I Am a River Driver"

"I Am a River Driver" from *Lumbering Songs from the Northern Woods* by Edith Fowke, Tunes transcribed by Norman Cazden.
Published for the American Folklore Society by the University of Texas Press, Austin and London: copyright 1970 by the American Folklore
Society Memoir Series, Wm. Hugh Jansen, General Editor, vol. 55, 1970.

2.   "How We Got Up to the Woods Last Year"

"How We Got Up to the Woods Last Year" from *Lumbering Songs from the Northern Woods* by Edith Fowke, Tunes transcribed by
Norman Cazden. Published for the American Folklore Society by the University of Texas Press, Austin and London: copyright 1970 by the
American Folklore Society Memoir Series, Wm. Hugh Jansen, General Editor, vol. 55, 1970.

3.   "The Raftsmen's Song"

"The Raftsmen's Song" from *Lumbering Songs from the Northern Woods* by Edith Fowke, Tunes transcribed by Norman Cazden.
Published for the American Folklore Society by the University of Texas Press, Austin and London: copyright 1970 by the American Folklore
Society Memoir Series, Wm. Hugh Jansen, General Editor, vol. 55, 1970.

4.   "Z'Basel an mym Rhy"

Songs 5–10 in this section include songs by the trouvéres of the twelfth and thirteenth century France—in chronological order: Richard the Lion-hearted (1157–1199); Gace Brulé (1160–1213); Lord of Couch (1165–1203); Thibaut IV, King of Navarre (1201–1253); Adam de la Hale (1235–1288). These melodies, including the one that is anonymous, are taken from the 1927 edition published by the University of Pennsylvania Press (printed in U. S. A. 1964), vol. II titled *L'Édition du Corpus Cantilenarum Medii Aevi*. The numbers that appear together with each song are those of the 1927 (1964 printing) edition.

5.

"Chanson de croisade" (Song from the Crusade)—1202 (fourth crusade) Lord of Couch (?), No. 326

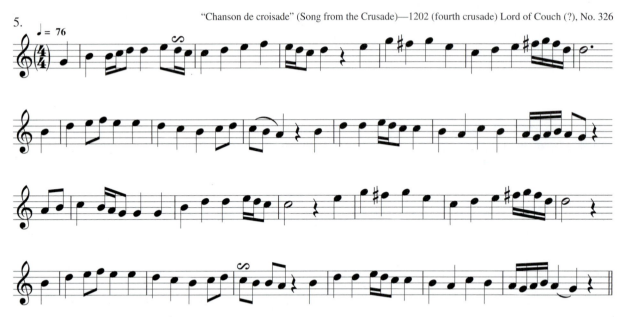

"Chanson de Croisade" (Song from the Crusade) No. 326 from *Les Chansonniers des Troubadours et des Trouvéres,* vol. 2, 1927. Reprinted by permission of the University of Pennsylvania Press.

6.

Thibaut IV, King of Navarre   "Pastorelle" (Pastoral), No. 142

"Pastorelle" No. 142 from *Les Chansonniers des Troubadours et des Trouvéres,* vol. 2, 1927. Reprinted by permission of the University of Pennsylvania Press.

7.

"Chanson" (Song) No. 152 from *Les Chansonniers des Troubadours et des Trouvéres,* vol. 2, 1927. Reprinted by permission of the University of Pennsylvania Press.

8.

Adam de la Hale   "Chanson" (Song), No. 112

"Chanson" (Song) No. 112 from *Les Chansonniers des Troubadours et des Trouvéres,* vol. 2, 1927. Reprinted by permission of the University of Pennsylvania Press.

9.

Gace Brulé   (?) "Chanson" (Song), No. 59

"Chanson" (Song) No. 59 from *Les Chansonniers des Troubadours et des Trouvéres,* vol. 2, 1927. Reprinted by permission of the University of Pennsylvania Press.

10.

Gace Brulé "Chanson" (Song), No. 60

"Chanson" (Song) No. 60 from *Les Chansonniers des Troubadours et des Trouvéres,* vol. 2, 1927. Reprinted by permission of the University of Pennsylvania Press.

D Melodies (Major and Minor): M6 and m6

SECTION 1. Robert Schumann

The melodies in this section are taken from instrumental works by Robert Schumann. The first two selections from Schumann's *Album for the Young,* op. 68, provide further exercises in clef reading.

Example 1:   This excerpt is in A B A form. The melody of the B section is almost the same as A except that it centers around G as tonic rather than C. With the return of the original material in the final A, the bass clef is used to illustrate the 5th relationship between the bass and tenor clefs. Sing these two lines an octave higher.

Example 2:   Line 2 is almost identical to line 1, except for its octave transposition, and allows you to check to see whether you are reading the clef correctly. The only new clef is the mezzo-soprano clef, which places middle C (c') on the second line up from the lowest.

1.   Schumann *Trällerliedchen* (Humming Tune), op. 68, no. 3

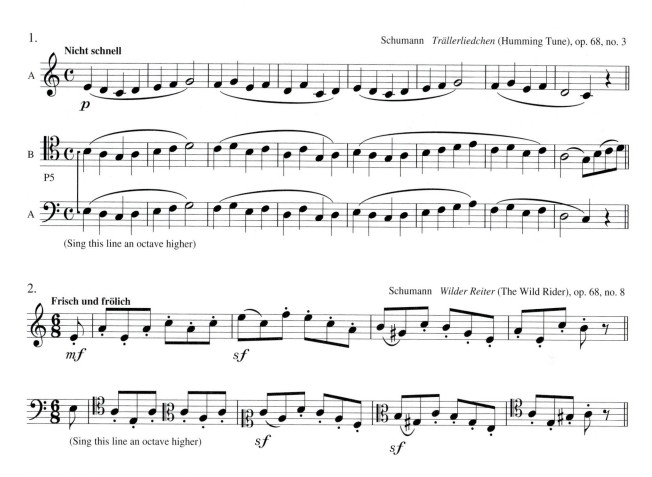

The clef reading strategies outlined for examples 1 and 2 should be applied to melodies 3–10, also by Schumann.

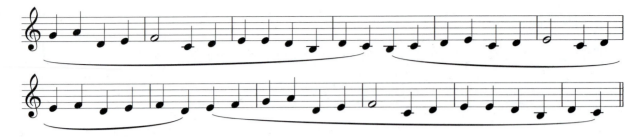

Schumann   #5 from *Albumblätter* (Album Leaves), op. 99, no. 8

6.

Schumann   *Scherzo* op. 99, no. 13

7.

Schumann   *Kleine Romanze* (Little Romance), op. 68, no. 19 (transposed) (abridged)

8.

Schumann   *Ernteliedchen* (Harvest Song), op. 68, no. 24 (transposed) (abridged)

9.

Schumann   *Schnitterliedchen* (The Reapers' Song), op. 68, no. 18

10.

SECTION 2. From Bach to Barber

The six melodies in this section are from works by various composers from Bach to Barber.

Transpose this familiar Rossini tune up a minor 2nd to F major, starting on note C, by reading in the alto clef (displaced by an octave).

1.   Rossini *William Tell* Overture, R-10

* Ten measures omitted

2.   Schubert *Ecossaise* I, D. 421

(mm. 1–4) * octave lower than original

3.   Bach   English Suite III, Gavotte II (or Musette)

*(eight measures omitted)

4.   Bach   Brandenburg Concerto no. 2, I (transposed down two octaves)

5. **In waltz time** ♩ = 112

Barber "Under the Willow Tree" from *Vanessa*

Barber *Bessie Bobtail*, op. 2, no. 3

6. **Andante, un poco moso** ♩ = 96

E Ensembles

SECTION 1. Ensemble Singing in Familiar Clefs

This section begins with settings of the *Kyrie* and *Christe* from the *Litany of the Blessed Virgin Mary* by Johann de Fossa together with the sources from Gregorian chant. (Other excerpts of chant were given in Unit 1 B, Section 2.) The other excerpt is from a work by Beethoven.

Johann de Fossa *Litania de B.V.M.* (Litany of the Blessed Virgin Mary)

1.

Ky - ri - e   e - lei - son.

Chri - ste _____ e - lei - son.

Chri - ste _____ e - lei - son.

Chri - ste _____ e - lei - son.

Chri - ste _____ e - lei - son.

Chri - ste _____ e - lei - son.

Ky - ri - e e - lei - son.

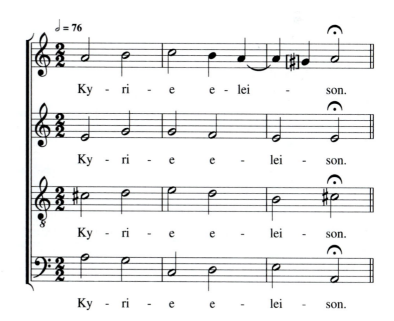

Ky - ri - e e - lei - son.

Ky - ri - e e - lei - son.

Ky - ri - e e - lei - son.

Ky - ri - e e - lei - son.

1. Chri - ste ____ au - di nos.
2. Chri - ste ex - au - di nos.

1. Chri - ste ____ au - di nos.
2. Chri - ste ex - au - di nos.

1. Chri - ste ____ au - di nos.
2. Chri - ste ex - au - di nos.

1. Chri - ste ____ au - di nos.
2. Chri - ste ex - au - di nos.

1. Chri - ste ____ au - di nos.
2. Chri - ste ex - au - di nos.

Adapted from *Litania de B.V.M.* by Johann de Fossa, and published in *Johann de Fossa: The Collected Works*, edited by Egbert M. Ennulat. Recent Researches in the Music of the Renaissance, vols. 28–29. Madison, Wisconsin: A-R Editions, Inc. 1978. Used with permission.

2.

Beethoven   Sonata for Piano and Cello op. 69, I (transposed from E major)

Allegro ma non tanto

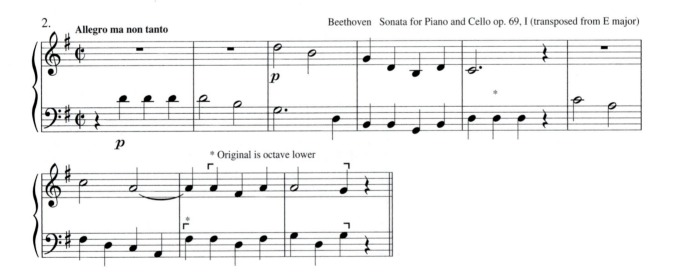

* Original is octave lower

SECTION 2. Ensemble Singing in Unfamiliar Clefs

The first excerpt is from a Mozart string quartet and can be used as a choral or instrumental exercise, or both.

1.

Mozart String Quartet, K. 458, I (transposed)

The second excerpt is related to the improvisation exercise introduced earlier in this unit (part B, section 4), based on the Tenor *David*. Here, you will find the same isorhythmic bass of 22 measures with two statements of the rhythmic *talea*. It serves as the accompaniment for the two-voice hocket by Machaut. For information about the cultural context for this work, students are invited to read Chapter 8: "Machaut's *David Hocket* and the coronation of Charles V (1364)" in a book titled *Guillaume de Machaut and Reims: Context and Meaning in His Musical Works,* by Ann Walters Robertson and published in 2002 by Cambridge University Press.

In 1981, Harrison Birtwistle wrote a modern arrangement of *Hoquetus David. Instrumental Motet. Guillaume de Machaut.*

Students should be encouraged to bring their instruments to class.

2.

Triplum

Hoquetus

Tenor
DAVID

I

II

Printed with the friendly permission of Breitkopf & Härtel, Wiesbaden.

UNIT SEVEN

A Rhythm—Review of Simple Meter with Emphasis on Irregular Division of the Beat: The Triplet

SECTION 1. Modules in Simple Meter

Using rhythm syllables or a neutral syllable, sing each of the given modules. Begin by repeating each module several times, then treat the successive modules as a continuous exercise.

Just as in the modules of unit 5, we are emphasizing the triplet, which represents an irregular division of the beat in simple meter.

SECTION 2. Phrases in Simple Meter with Irregular Division of the Beat: The Triplet

For numbers 1–4, follow the procedures outlined in unit 1A, section 2. For the two-part exercises (5–6), follow the procedures outlined in unit 2A, section 2.

5.

6. Rhythmic canon

This ensemble passage is taken from a larger work titled "Quitta Mouille" for two drums and is representative of Haitian drumming. For further information see "Drum Music for Two Dances," chapter 7 in *Haiti Singing,* by Harold Courlander (Chapel Hill: University of North Carolina Press, 1939).

Quitta Mouille

♩ = 132

1st drum

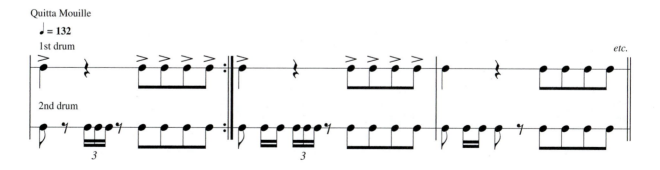

2nd drum

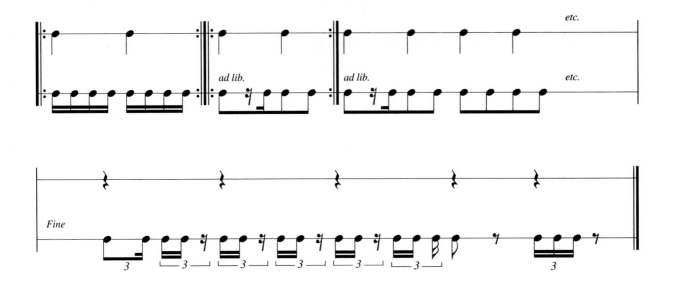

SECTION 3. Creating a Coherent Phrase in Simple Meter

Return to section 1 and select three or four rhythm modules. Place them in an order that creates a coherent four-measure phrase.

Write your solution on the following line:

B Diatonic Models and Melodic Fragments for Interval Singing—New Interval: m7

SECTION 1. Diatonic Models

The exercises in this section relate to the music of Haydn, Mozart, and Beethoven, with particular emphasis on the minor 7th. The musical fragments that correspond with these exercises are quoted in section 2.

The two models that follow are related to the Haydn and Mozart fragments (nos. 1 and 2). Treat these models as exercises in antiphonal singing by having half the class sing "a" and the other half answer by singing "b." Continue this process in all major keys, transposing to each new key by P5s down or P4s up.

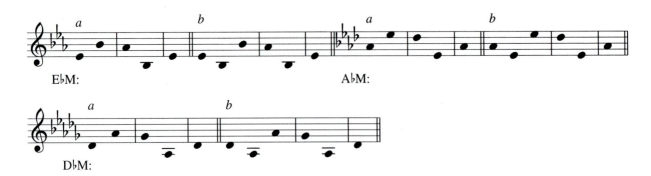

Follow the same principle of antiphonal singing with the next model. Letter "a" represents fragment 3 (Mozart's Horn Concerto, K. 447, first movement); "b" represents fragment 4 from the third movement of the same concerto.

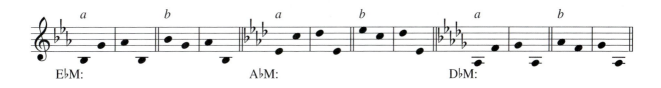

Here is another model for antiphonal singing. Letter "a" corresponds with fragment 5 (from the second movement of the same horn concerto as fragments 3 and 4); "b" corresponds with fragment 6 from another Mozart horn concerto (K. 447, second movement).

This model follows the contour of fragment 7 (Haydn) and fragment 8 (Beethoven). Sing the model in all major keys.

The last three melodic fragments (9, 10, and 11) in the next section are further illustrations of the patterns already presented.

SECTION 2. Melodic Fragments in E♭ Major

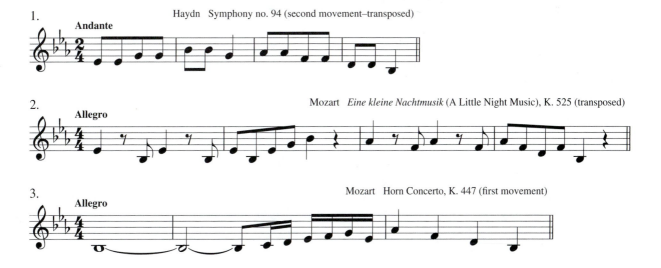

1.

Haydn   Symphony no. 94 (second movement–transposed)

Andante

2.

Mozart   *Eine kleine Nachtmusik* (A Little Night Music), K. 525 (transposed)

Allegro

3.

Mozart   Horn Concerto, K. 447 (first movement)

Allegro

SECTION 3. Creating a Coherent Melody

Return to section 2 and select two or three segments of melodic fragments that create a coherent melody. It may be necessary to change the meter and rhythm of certain segments, depending on your choice.

SECTION 4. Improvisation

The following vocalise pattern will be expanded in subsequent chapters and will eventually become the basis for improvisation exercises that modulate. For now, study the harmonic implications of this pattern and use it as a model for analyzing Mozart's use of V^7–I in excerpts from *The Magic Flute* (transposed to C). Improvise a melodic pattern in the spirit of one of the excerpts from *The Magic Flute*.

Improvise a pattern in the spirit of one of the excerpts from *The Magic Flute*.

C   Melodies (Major and Minor): M6 and m6

SECTION 1. Melodies from Songs and Instrumental Works by Beethoven

The melodies in this section are from instrumental and vocal works by Beethoven.

Beethoven   Two Sonatinas, I (transposed)

1.

Beethoven   Two Sonatinas, I *Romanze* (transposed)

2.
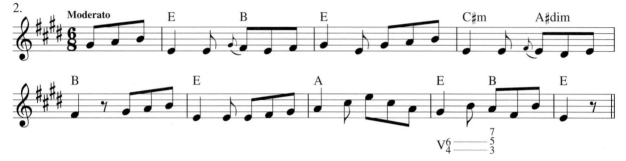

Beethoven   Three Sonatas, no. 3, II, Var. II, WoO 47

3.

Beethoven   Three Sonatas, no.3, Var. VI, WoO 47

4.

Beethoven   *Urians Reise um die Welt* (Urian's Journey Round the World), op. 52, no. 1

5. **In einer massigen geschwinden Bewegung mit einer komischen Art gesungen**

Beethoven *Das Glück der freundschaft* (The Joy of Friendship), op. 88

Beethoven *Der Mann von Wort* (A Man of His Word), op. 99 (transposed)

SECTION 2. Short Melodies

These short melodies will provide the opportunity for rapid reading of melodic patterns that are typical of music of the common practice period.

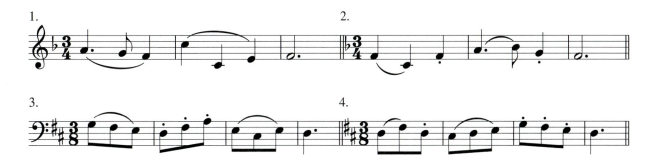

D Melodies (Major and Minor): M6 and m6

The melodies in this section are taken from instrumental works by George Friedrich Händel. The HWV numbers are from the reference manual of the *Händel-Handbuch* (vol. 3), published by Bärenreiter Kassel, Basel and London, 1986.

1. Handel *Wassermusik* (Water Music), Suite no. 2 in D Major, 12 *Alla Hornpipe*, HWV 349 (transposed)

2. Handel *Wassermusik* (Water Music), Suite no. 1 in F Major, 8 *Bourrée*, HWV 348 (transposed)
    Presto

3. Handel   Suite no. 7 in B♭ Major, *Gigue*, HWV 440

4. Handel *Wassermusik* (Water Music), Suite no. 1 in F Major, 4, HWV 348 (transposed)
    Andante

5.

Handel   Suite no. 1 in B♭ Major, *Menuet,* HWV 434 (transposed octave lower)

6.

Handel   Suite no. 9 in G Major, *Chaconne,* HWV 442 (transposed)

Fine

D.C.

7.

Handel   Suite no. 8 in G Major, *Gigue,* HWV 441

8.

Handel   Suite no. 3 in D Minor, Var. 4, HWV 428

9.

Handel Suite no. 4 in D Minor, *Sarabande,* Var. 1, HWV 437

Handel Suite no. 5 in E Major, *Air,* "The Harmonious Blacksmith" HWV 430

10.

E Ensembles

SECTION 1. Ensemble Singing in Familiar Clefs

These excerpts are from works by Handel, Couperin, Haydn, and Bach.

Handel Suite no. 9 in G Major, Var. 62, HWV 442 (transposed)

1.

2.

This is an interesting excerpt because, according to the directions, it may be sung forward and backward, then turned upside down and sung both forward and backward. The text translates freely: "You should dedicate yourself entirely to your art."

Haydn   Die Zehn Gebote der Kunst (The Ten Commandments of Art), no. 1 "Du sollst dich ganz der Kunst weihen" (You should dedicate yourself entirely to your art)

3.

Transpose this familiar melody down a major 2nd to G by reading the upper line in tenor clef (for these purposes, the fourth line is c", an 8ve higher than c') and the lower line in alto clef (for these purposes, the middle line is c, an 8ve lower than c').

4.

Inner voices omitted

SECTION 2. Ensemble Singing in Unfamiliar Clefs

This excerpt will be continued in unit 8E-2.

Bach Motet 3 *Jesu, meine Freude* (Jesus, Priceless Treasure), BWV 227

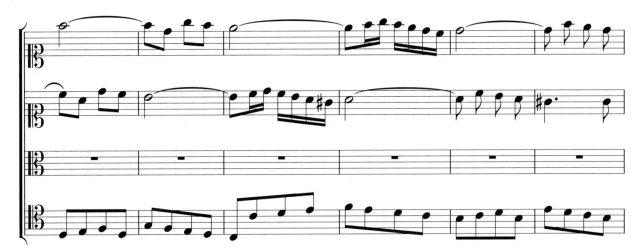

371 HARMONIZED CHORALES AND 69 CHORALE MELODIES by Johann S. Bach. Edited by Albert Riemenschneider. Copyright © 1941 (Renewed) by G. Schirmer, Inc. (ASCAP). International Copyright Secured. All Rights Reserved. Reprinted by permission.

UNIT EIGHT

A Rhythm—Review of Simple Meter and Compound Meter

SECTION 1. Modules in Simple Meter

Follow the procedures given in the previous units.

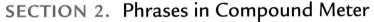

SECTION 2. Phrases in Compound Meter

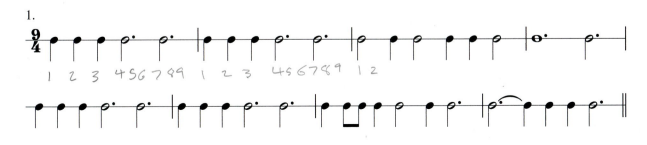

8. Oricha Oko

Adapted from *The Music of Santería*, pp. 91–92. *Traditional Rhythms of the Bata Drums,* by John Amira and Steven Cornelius (Crown Point, Ind.: White Cliffs Media Company, 1992).

SECTION 3. Creating a Coherent Phrase in Simple or Compound Meter

Return to section 1 and select three or four rhythm modules. Place them in an order that creates a coherent four-measure phrase.

Write your solution on the following line:

B Diatonic Models and Melodic Fragments for Interval Singing—New Interval: M7

SECTION 1. Diatonic Models

The exercises in this section relate to the music of Verdi, Stravinsky, Wagner, Bach, and Beethoven with particular emphasis on the minor 7th (m7). The musical fragments that correspond with these exercises are quoted in section 2.

The first model (in minor) is related to the first melodic fragment (Bach); the second model (in major) is related to fragments 2 and 3 by Wagner. Sing the first model in keys a minor 3rd above (i.e., C, E♭, F♯), then sing the next model in keys a minor 3rd below (E♭, C, A, and so on).

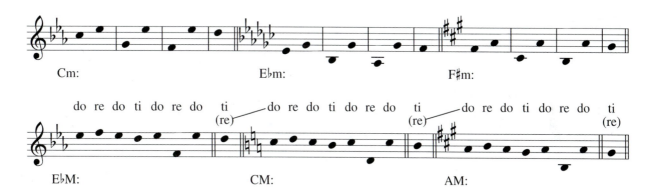

If you find it difficult to sing the second model in keys separated by a minor 3rd, the reason is that the melodic patterns combine to form a segment of the octatonic scale (i.e., a scale of alternating major and minor seconds). See the following model:

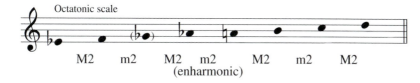

Only two models are necessary to introduce the major 7th (M7) from E♭ to D. These are preparatory materials for melodic fragments 5–7.

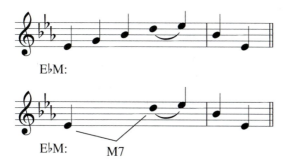

Only two models are necessary to introduce the major 7th (M7, from A♭ to G) as preparation for melodic fragments 8 and 9. The second model is almost the reverse of the first.

These models are quite similar to the previous two, except that they are in minor keys. For those who want to emphasize relative relationships, C minor is provided; for those who prefer parallel relationships, E♭ minor is available. These models are in preparation for melodic fragments 10, 10a, 11, and 11a in the next section.

SECTION 2. Melodic Fragments in C Minor, E♭ Major, and E♭ Minor

6.   Stravinsky *Petrushka* (transposed)

PETROUCHKA (Stravinsky) © Copyright 1912 by Hawkes & Son (London) Ltd. Copyright Renewed. Reprinted by permission of Boosey & Hawkes, Inc.

7.   Beethoven Piano Sonata op. 10, no. 3 (first movement—transposed)

8.   Bach French Suite no. 6, *Allemande* (transposed)

9.   Bach Partita no. 2, *Rondeau*

10a.   Bach French Suite no. 3, *Sarabande* (transposed)

10b.   Bach French Suite no. 3, *Sarabande* (transposed)

11a.   Bach *Well-Tempered Clavier,* Book I, Fugue 10 (transposed)

11b.   Bach *Well-Tempered Clavier,* Book I, Fugue 10 (transposed)

12a.   Bach *Die Kunst der Fuge* (Art of Fugue), no. 9 (transposed)

12b.

Bach *Die Kunst der Fuge* (Art of Fugue), no. 9 (transposed)

13a.

Bach English Suite no. 5, *Gigue* (transposed)

13b.

Bach English Suite no. 5, *Gigue* (transposed)

SECTION 3. Creating a Coherent Melody

Return to section 2 and select two or three segments of melodic fragments that would create a coherent melody. It may be necessary to change the meter and rhythm of certain segments, depending on your choice.

SECTION 4. Improvisation

The following vocalise pattern that was introduced in unit 7-B-4 is now being expanded to include all inversions of the dominant seventh chord. Students should eventually memorize this expanded vocalise pattern.

Use the "expanded vocalise pattern" as the basis for an improvisation. Begin by taking one of the fragments from *The Magic Flute* in unit 7-B-4 and follow the "roadmap" of the expanded vocalise pattern. After you have established the linear harmonies for your improvisation, try to embellish these harmonies by dividing the quarter notes into eighth notes and by using as much stepwise motion as possible. Here is an example, using melody #2 as sung by Monostratos:

C Melodies (Major and Minor): m7

SECTION 1. Melodies from Operas by Verdi, Puccini, Handel, and Pergolesi

The melodies in this section are from operas by Verdi, Puccini, Handel, and Pergolesi.

4.
Allegro giusto ♩ = 100
Cantabile dolcissimo

Verdi   Duet from *Aida*, act III Aida and Amonasro

Amonasro

5.
Allegro giusto ♩ = 100

Verdi   Duet from *Aida*, act III Aida and Radames

Radames

6.
Andantino ingenuo ♪ = 120
dolce

Puccini   *Gianni Schicchi*, R–40 (transposed)

Lauretta

7.
Largo

Handel   *Julius Caesar*, act I

Cleopatra

8.
Andante ♩ = 60

Verdi   *Attila*, act II, R–85

Ezio

9. **Allegro giusto** ♩ = 108

Ezio

G. B. Pergolesi *La Serva Padrona* (The Servant Landlady), act I, Aria

10. **Allegro assai**

Uberto
Pandolphe

SECTION 2. Excerpts from Cantatas Written by J. S. Bach

The excerpts in this section are taken from the cantatas of J. S. Bach.

1. ♩ = 88 — Cantata no. 4

2. ♩ = 88 — Cantata no. 5

3. ♩ = 88 — Cantata no. 46

4. ♩ = 88 — Cantata no. 42

5. ♩ = 88 — Cantata no. 72

6.   Cantata no. 75

7.   Cantata no. 89

8.   Cantata no. 144

9.   Cantata no. 189

10.   Cantata no. 197

D Melodies (Major and Minor): m7

SECTION 1. Folk Songs from the U.S. Northern Woods and Haiti, Melodies from Instrumental Works by Bach and Bruckner

The first six melodies in this section are from folk song collections of the northern woods of the United States and of Haiti and emphasize some of the most complicated rhythm patterns presented thus far. The next six melodies are from the keyboard literature of Bach. The last 2 melodies are from Bruckner's Fifth Symphony, second movement.

The juxtaposition of the Bruckner excerpts with those from the *Art of Fugue* in this section, as well as in the subsequent part E, "Ensembles," gives evidence of Bruckner's homage to this monumental work by Bach.

1.   "Driving Saw-Logs on the Plover"

"Driving Saw-Logs on the Plover" from *Lumbering Songs from the Northern Woods* by Edith Fowke, tunes transcribed by Norman Cazden. Published for the American Folklore Society by the University of Texas Press, Austin and London: Copyright 1970 by the American Folklore Society Memoir Series, Wm. Hugh Jansen, General Editor, vol. 55, 1970.

2.   "Save Your Money While You're Young"

"Save Your Money While You're Young" from *Lumbering Songs from the Northern Woods* by Edith Fowke, tunes transcribed by Norman Cazden. Published for the American Folklore Society by the University of Texas Press, Austin and London: Copyright 1970 by the American Folklore Society Memoir Series, Wm. Hugh Jansen, General Editor, vol. 55, 1970.

3.   Haiti   "St. Jacques pastà"

4.   Haiti   "Fai Ogoun"

12.

13. **Sehr langsam**
dolce

Bruckner Symphony no. 5, II

oboe

14. **Sehr langsam**

Bruckner Symphony no. 5, II

cello

E Ensembles

SECTION 1. Ensemble Singing in Familiar Clefs

1.
Adagio

Haydn *Gott im Herzen* (To Have God in One's Heart)

Bach *Die Kunst der Fuge* (Art of Fugue), Contrapunctus V

2.

Beethoven WoO 50, II

3. **Allegretto**

* See unit 9B for d5.

4. Voices

Beethoven WoO 192

Ars lon - ga, vi - ta bre - vis.

5. Voices

Beethoven WoO 193

Ars lon - ga, vi - ta bre - vis.

6.

Beethoven WoO 191

B - A - C - H

Kühl, ___ nicht lau, nicht lau, kühl, ___ nicht lau, kühl, ___ nicht lau.

Kül, ___ nicht lau, kühl, ___ nicht lau, nicht lau.

Kühl, ___ nicht lau, kühl, ___ nicht lau, kühl, ___ nicht lau.

SECTION 2. Ensemble Singing in Unfamiliar Clefs

This excerpt is continued from unit 7E-2.

Bach Motet 3, *Jesu, meine Freude* (Jesus, Priceless Treasure), BWV 227

371 HARMONIZED CHORALES AND 69 CHORALE MELODIES By Johann S. Bach. Edited by Albert Riemenschneider. Copyright © 1941 (Renewed) by G. Schirmer, Inc. (ASCAP). International Copyright Secured. All Rights Reserved. Reprinted by permission.

UNIT NINE

A Rhythm—Compound Meter: Subdivision of the Beat

SECTION 1. Modules in Compound Meter

Using rhythm syllables or a neutral syllable, sing each of the given modules. Begin by repeating each module several times, then treat the successive modules as a continuous exercise.

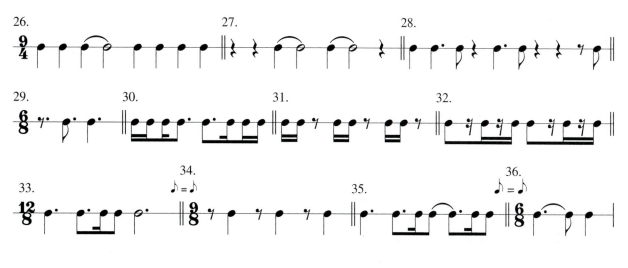

SECTION 2. Phrases in Simple and Compound Meters with Triple Subdivisions

5.

6. Rhythmic canon

SECTION 3. Creating a Coherent Phrase in Compound Meter

Return to section 1 and select three or four rhythm modules. Place them in an order that creates a coherent four-measure phrase.

Write your solution on the following line:

B Diatonic Models and Melodic Fragments for Interval Singing—New Intervals: A4 and d5

SECTION 1. Diatonic Models

The exercises in this section relate to the melodic fragments of Bach, Beethoven, and Mozart.

The following examples emphasize the resolution of the diminished 5th (d5; D♯–A) to the major 3rd (M3; E–G♯), as given in the following model:

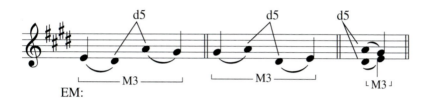

Learning to sing the exercises derived from this excerpt will help you understand the intricacies of voice leading involved in the treatment of tritones. Most often, successive melodic tritones are harmonized by dominant 7th chords, moving sequentially downward by P5s. Sing the following model in all major keys, transposing to each new key by P5s down or P4s up, as shown in the following model:

Try the following accelerated method for traveling through the various keys.

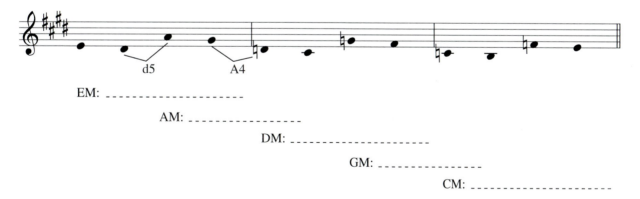

EM: _

AM: _ _ _ _ _ _ _ _ _ _ _ _ _ _ _ _ _ _

DM: _

GM: _ _ _ _ _ _ _ _ _ _ _ _ _ _ _ _ _ _

CM: _

This model shows the resolution of the augmented 4th (A4; F♯–B♯) to the major 6th (M6; E–C♯) and is related to fragment 6.

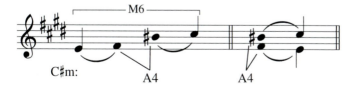

The next series of models (indicated as 7a–b–12a–b) relate to the Bach chorales in the next section. For those who are learning La-based minor, sing 7a–12a. If your instructor prefers Do-based minor, sing 7b–12b. If fixed La or chromatic fixed Do is the preference, you should sing both types of models (7a–12b).

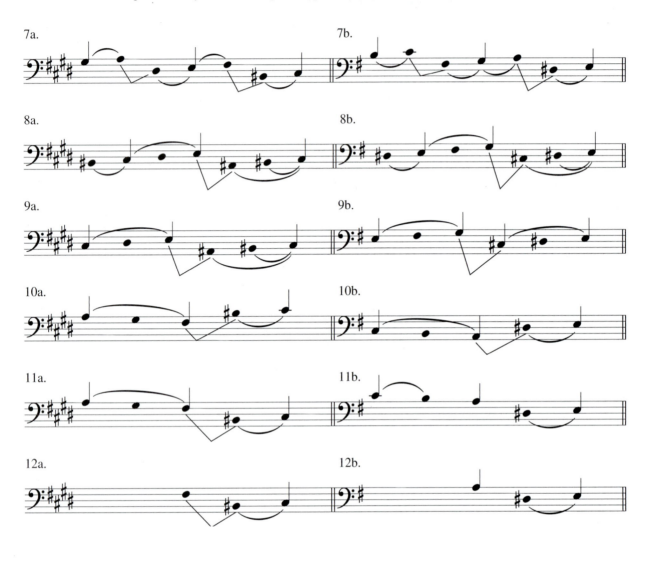

SECTION 2. Melodic Fragments in E Major (C♯ Minor and E Minor)

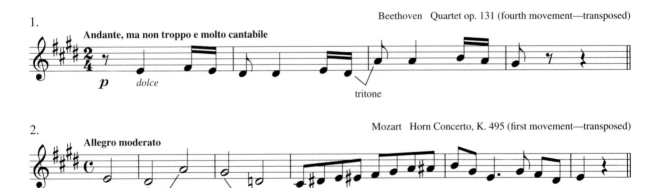

For convenience, the Riemenschneider numbers are used to identify fragments 7–10.

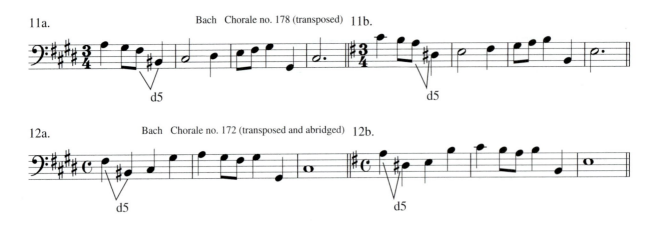

11a.   Bach   Chorale no. 178 (transposed)   11b.

d5   d5

12a.   Bach   Chorale no. 172 (transposed and abridged)   12b.

d5   d5

Supplemental fragments emphasizing secondary leading-tone [L.T.] functions.

Beethoven   Symphony no. 1, op. 21, I (m. 1–4 transposed from C major)

13.   **Adagio molto** ♪ = 88
[L.T.]   4̂   L.T.   1̂   [L.T.]   5̂
EM: d5   A4

Beethoven   Symphony no. 1, op. 21 (mm. 41–45 abridged and transposed)

14.   **Allegro con brio** ♩ = 112
L.T. 1̂ [L.T.] 2̂   [L.T.] 3̂ [L.T.] 4̂   [L.T.] 5̂
EM:

SECTION 3. Creating a Coherent Melody

Return to section 2 and select two or three segments of melodic fragments that create a coherent melody. It may be necessary to change the meter and rhythm of certain segments, depending on your choice.

SECTION 4. Improvisation

The vocalise pattern that was introduced in unit 7-B-4 is now extended to include modulatory patterns. Be mindful of the thin line that exists between modulation and tonicization. These modulatory patterns can be shaped to produce a modulation or a tonicization, depending on the context that you establish in your improvisation.

Modulatory patterns from C major to G major (The first exercise is structured according to the basic vocalise pattern; the second one is more free to encourage you to create your own modulatory improvisation.)

1. I to V

to V

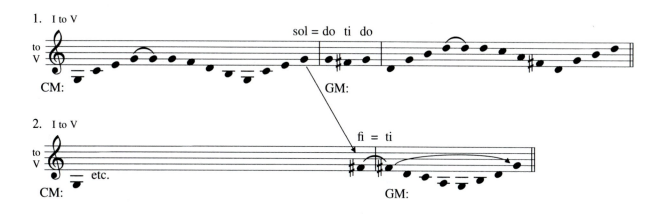

sol = do ti do

CM:
GM:

2. I to V

to V

fi = ti

CM:
GM:

Modulatory patterns from C major to F major

3. I to IV

to IV

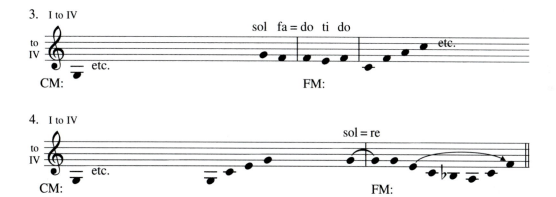

sol fa = do ti do

etc.

CM:
FM:

4. I to IV

to IV

sol = re

CM:
FM:

Modulatory patterns from C minor to G minor

5. i to v

to v

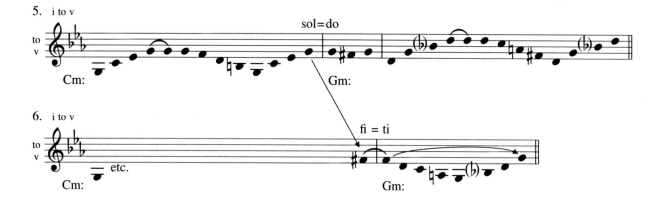

sol = do

Cm:
Gm:

6. i to v

to v

fi = ti

Cm:
Gm:

Modulatory patterns from C minor to F minor

7. i to iv

to iv

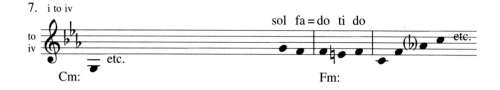

sol fa = do ti do

etc.

Cm:
Fm:

8. i to iv

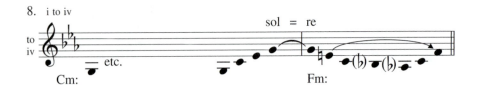

The following work is listed as "doubtful" in terms of authorship, even though it is designated as BWV 517 among all the works by Bach. Within the framework of F major, this anonymous composer has raised scale degree 4 (from B♭ to B♮) and lowered scale degree 7 (from E♮ to E♭ created) creating tonicizations of V and IV. These are the same alterations that you experienced in modulatory patterns 1–4 above.

9.

Bach? *Wie wohl ist mir, o Freund der Seelen* (Blessed Am I, Friend of My Soul), BWV 517 (anon.)

? Wie wohl ist mir, o Freund der Seelen from *Notebook for Anna Magdalena Bach* by Bach; no. 5. Copyright © 1968 Barenreiter-Verlag-Kassel. Reprinted by permission.

The modulatory patterns outlined in exercises 5–8 above are implied in the following melody in D minor. For a full harmonization, consult an edition of Bach's Sacred Songs.

10.

Bach *Der Tag mit seinem Lichte* (The Day with Its Light), BWV 448

Der Tag mit seinem Lichte from *Notebook for Anna Magdalena Bach* by Bach; no. 4 Schmellis Gesanguch. Copyright © 1968 Barenreiter-Verlag-Kassel. Reprinted by permission.

Using numbers 9 and 10 as models, you are now invited to improvise two melodies.

C Melodies (Major): Chromatic Alterations, Modulating, and Nonmodulating

The melodies in this section are excerpts from the Mozart song literature. These excerpts were transposed to the key of C major for ease in seeing and hearing notes outside the diatonic framework. Examples include alterations of the following scale degrees: 4 (F♯), 2 (D♯), 5 (G♯), and 1 (C♯). These exercises are designed to assist you with the Mozart songs in the next part of this unit.

5. Mozart *Die Zufriedenheit* (Contentment), K. 349/367a (last phrase transposed from G to C)

6. Mozart *An die Einsamkeit* (In Solitude), K. 391/340b (mm. 7–13 transposed from B♭ to C)

7. Mozart *Gesellenreise (Freimaurerlied)* [Life's Journey (Song of the Freemason)], K. 468
(mm. 1–2 transposed from B♭ to C)

8. Mozart *Des kleinen Friedrichs Geburtstag* (Little Frederick's Birthday), K. 529
(last 2 mm. transposed from F to C)

9. Mozart *Zum Schluss* (At the End), K. 484 (last phrase transposed from G to C)

10. Mozart *Die Verschweigung* (Discretion), K. 518 (mm. 10–17 transposed from F to C)

D Melodies (Major): Chromatic Alterations, Modulating, and Nonmodulating

SECTION 1. Mozart Songs

The melodies in this section are taken from the Mozart song literature.

Not all of the melodies contain modulations, but in addition to the possibility of modulations, melodies in this part may also include chromatic alterations because of one or another of the following: (1) accompaniments with secondary dominant or leading-tone harmonies; (2) accompaniments with other chromatic harmonies, such as borrowed chords, augmented 6ths, and Neapolitan 6ths; and (3) chromatic nonharmonic tones.

Your instructor will provide directions for the use of syllables or numbers as they relate to the sources of alteration.

1.

Mozart *Das Kinderspiel* (Children's Games), K. 598 (transposed)

2.

Mozart *Warnung* (A Warning), K. 433/416c

3.

Mozart *Gesellenreise (Freimaurerlied)* [Life's Journey (Song of the Freemason)], K. 468

Mozart *Die Zufriedenheit* (Contentment), K. 473

4.
Calmato

Mozart *Sehnsucht nach dem Frülinge* (Longing for Spring), K. 596 (transposed)

5.
Giocoso

*d4

*See unit 13, part B, for d4.

Mozart *Im Frühlingsanfang* (At Spring's Outset), K. 597

6.
Un poco più lento

Mozart *An Chloe* (To Chloe, 2nd half of song), K. 524 (transposed)

7.

Allegretto

Mozart *Un moto di Gioja* (A Surge of Joy, 2nd half of song), K. 579 (abridged)

8. **Allegretto moderato**

Mozart *Die Verschweigung* (Discretion), K. 518

9. **No tempo given**

Mozart *Abendempfindung* (Evening Song, 2nd half of song), K. 523

10.

SECTION 2. Melodies from Eighteenth-Century Opera by Rameau and Pergolesi

This section includes three melodies from eighteenth-century opera. The first two solo excerpts are sung by Émilie in Rameau's opera-ballet *Les Indes galants* (The Courtly Indies), first performed on August 23, 1735. The third excerpt is sung by Aquilio in Pergolesi's *Adriano in Syria,* which was first performed on October 25, 1734. This aria became one of the sources for Stravinsky's *Pulcinella Ballet.* The specific example in the Stravinsky ballet begins at rehearsal 61, "ancora poco meno," ♩ = 86.

1.

Rameau *Les Indes galantes* (The Courtly Indies) Émilie

Rameau *Les Indes galantes* (The Courtly Indies) Émilie

2. **Tempête**

Pergolesi *Adriano in Syria,* Aria: *Contento forse vivere nel mio martir potrei* (Perhaps I Could Live Happily in My Misery) (abridged)

3. **Andante**

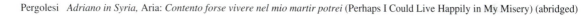

Contento forse vivere from *Adriano in Syria* by Pergolesi in *Complete Works/Opere Complete,* B. Brook, F. Degrada, & H. Hucke, eds. Co-sponsored by the Pergolesi Research Center, City University of New York, and the city of Iesi. Reprinted by permission of Pendragon Press.

E Ensembles

SECTION 1. Ensemble Singing in Familiar Clefs

The first example is the eighth canon from a group of ten written by Haydn, titled *Die Heiligen Zehn Gebote als Canons* (The Ten Commandments).

1.   Haydn *Achtes Gebote* (The Eighth Commandment)

Joseph Haydn Werke XXXI, Die heiligen Zehn Gebote, no. 8. © 1959 by G. Henle Verlag, Muenchen, used by permission.

2. Mozart *Terzettino* (Trio): *Soave sia il vento* (May Breezes Blow Lightly), from *Così fan Tutte* (All Women Do the Same), K. 588, no. 10

SECTION 2. Ensemble Singing in an Unfamiliar Clef

The following canons were written by Mozart in 1782 in Vienna. Both are based on texts by Hölty. The first is for two voices (K.V. 230 or K. 382b) and is titled "Elegie beim Grabe meinen Vaters" ("Elegy at the Grave of my Father"). The second is for three voices (K.V. 229 or K. 382a) and is titled "Auf den Tod einer Nachtigall" ("On the Death of a Nightingale").

For the convenience of the student and the instructor, two different formats are given. On the left-hand page, the unfamiliar soprano clefs are preserved. On the right-hand page, the same work is presented in the more familiar treble clefs. Treat these canons as sources for continuous drilling throughout the semester. You might want to begin with the familiar treble clef at first and then come back to the soprano clef when it becomes more familiar.

Mozart *Selig, selig, alle, alle* [Blessed, Blessed All, All (Who Sleep in the Lord)] Canon for 2 Voices, K. 230

1a. ♩ = 88

1b.

2a.

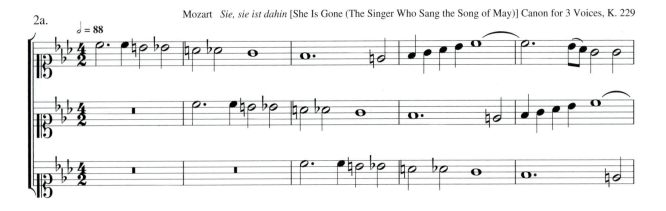

2b.

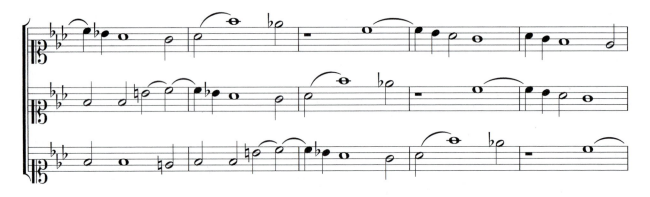

UNIT TEN

A Rhythm—Simple Meter: Mixed Meters and Irregular Division of the Beat

Use the conducting patterns shown below, if your instructor recommends you do so.

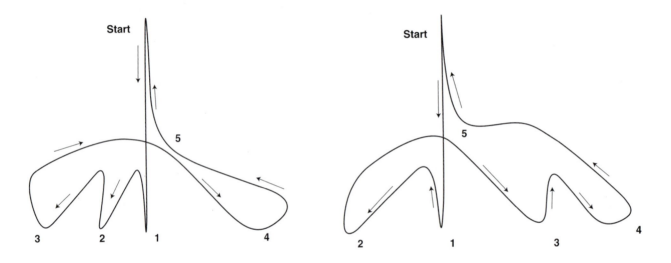

SECTION 1. Modules in Simple Meter

Using rhythm syllables or a neutral syllable, sing each of the given modules. Begin by repeating each module several times, then treat the successive modules as a continuous exercise.

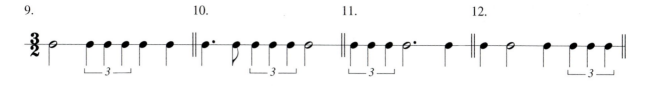

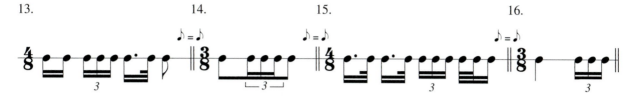

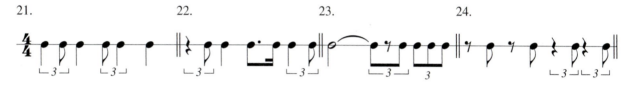

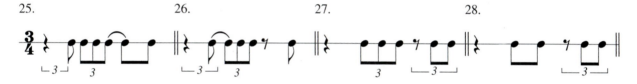

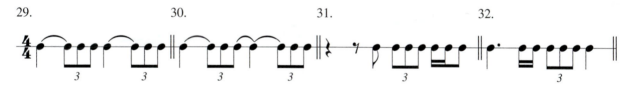

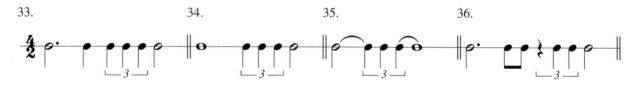

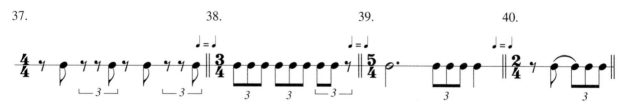

SECTION 2. Phrases in Simple Meter with Triplets

6. Rhythmic canon

7. Rhythmic ostinato

8. Rhythmic hocket

SECTION 3. Creating a Coherent Phrase in Simple Meter

Return to section 1 and select three or four rhythm modules. Place them in an order that creates a coherent four-measure phrase.

Write your solution on the following line:

_____ ‖

B Diatonic and Chromatic Models and Melodic Fragments for Interval Study—Review: A4 and d5

SECTION 1. Diatonic and Chromatic Models

As in the previous unit, these exercises focus on the tritone. In this unit, however, the models are based on fragments by a different set of composers: Wagner, Stravinsky, Franck, Mussorgsky, Debussy, Schubert, and Barber. Many of these models are extracted from highly chromatic textures, but the exercises themselves are mostly diatonic. Often the notes of resolution associated with the tritone, in traditional terms, are partially or fully absent in some exercises. The unifying thread that runs throughout part B of this unit is the pitch-specific nature of the tritone D♯–A. The one exception occurs in melodic fragments 9–11, where the transposition to relative minor changes D♯–A to F♯–C.

Follow the same procedure as in previous units. Sing the following model in all major keys.

EM: AM: DM:

The following table indicates how the models (in this section) relate to the fragments in section 2.

Models	Fragments
1 & 2	1 & 2
3	3
4	2
5	5
6	4
7	6
8	7
9	8
10	9
11	10

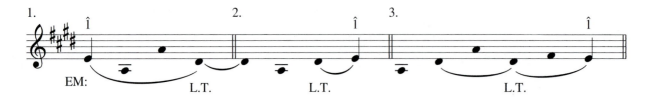

The following model shows how a tritone (A–D♯) is filled in with a M3 (A–C♯) and a M2 (C♯–D♯). The next model shows how the same tritone is approached by a M2 (B–A) and left by a M3 (D♯–B).

The next three models feature a tritone that is not filled in.

These models relate to fragments 9, 10, and 11 of the next section.

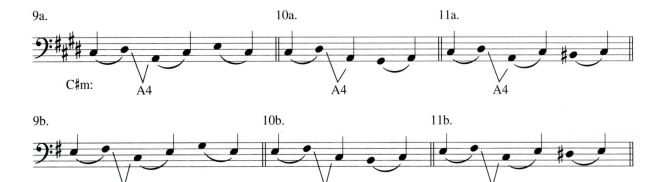

SECTION 2. Melodic Fragments in E Major (C♯ Minor and E Minor)

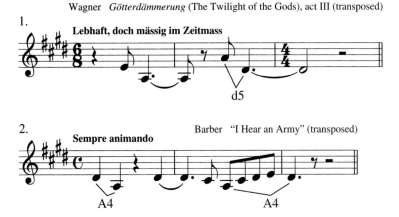

3.   Stravinsky *Petrouchka,* (transposed)

Lento cantabile

A4   d5   d5

PETROUCHKA (Stravinsky) © Copyright 1912 by Hawkes & Son (London) Ltd. Copyright Renewed. Reprinted by permission of Boosey & Hawkes, Inc.

4.   Wagner *Götterdämmerung,* act III, scene iii

Feierlich

A4   A4

Franck Violin Sonata for Violin and Piano (second movement—transposed)

5.

Allegro

A4

6. Debussy *Des femmes de Paris* (The Dames of Paris),
    from *Three Ballads of François Villon,* III (transposed)

Expressif et moqueur

A4

7.   Wagner *Götterdämmerung,* act III, scene iii (transposed)

Feierlich

d5

Mussorgsky *Boris Godunov,* act I, scene i (transposed)

8a.

Andante tranquillo

C♯m: A4

8b.   Mussorgsky *Boris Godunov,* act I, scene i (transposed)

Em: A4

9a.

Schubert *Ihr Bild* (Her Picture) (transposed)

C#m:

A4

9b.

Schubert *Ihr Bild* (Her Picture) (transposed)

Em:

A4

10a.

Barber "Rain Has Fallen" (transposed)

C#m:

A4

10b.

Barber "Rain Has Fallen" (transposed)

Em:

A4

RAIN HAS FALLEN from *Three Songs*, op. 10. By Samuel Barber. Copyright © 1939 (Renewed) by G. Schirmer, Inc. (ASCAP) International Copyright Secured. All Rights Reserved. Reprinted by Permission.

SECTION 3. Creating a Coherent Melody

Return to section 2 and select two or three segments of melodic fragments that create a coherent melody. It may be necessary to change the meter and rhythm of certain segments, depending on your choice.

SECTION 4. Improvisation

Refer to unit 9-B-4 if you have questions about "modulatory patterns" from tonic to dominant or subdominant in major and minor keys. In this section, we will focus on modulatory patterns from tonic to mediant, supertonic or submediant in major and minor keys, as well as tonic to subtonic in minor keys.

Modulatory patterns from C major to E minor

1. I to iii

to
iii

sol mi = do

etc.

etc.

CM:

Em:

2. I to iii

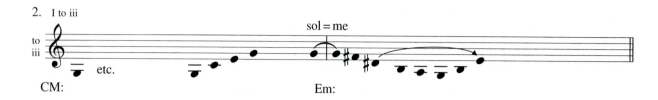

CM:　　　　　　　　　Em:

Modulatory patterns from C major to D minor

3. I to ii

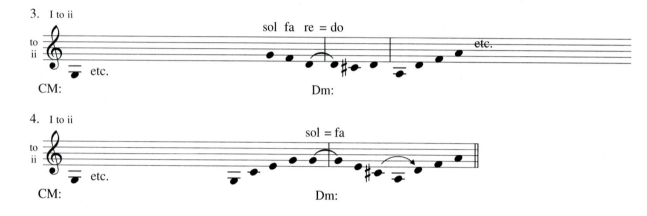

CM:　　　　　　　　　Dm:

4. I to ii

CM:　　　　　　　　　Dm:

Modulatory patterns from C minor to E-flat major

5. i to III

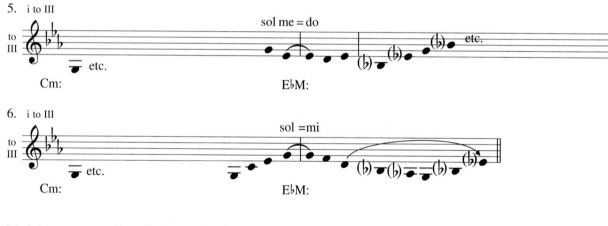

Cm:　　　　　　　　　E♭M:

6. i to III

Cm:　　　　　　　　　E♭M:

Modulatory patterns from C minor to D minor

7. i to ii

Cm:　　　　　　　　　Dm:

8. i to ii

Cm:　　　　　　　　　Dm:

Modulatory patterns from C major to A minor

9. I to vi

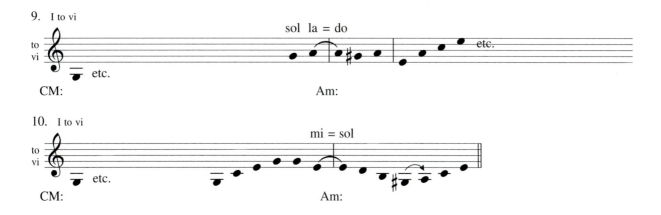

sol la = do

CM: Am:

10. I to vi

mi = sol

CM: Am:

Modulatory patterns from C minor to A-flat major

11. i to VI

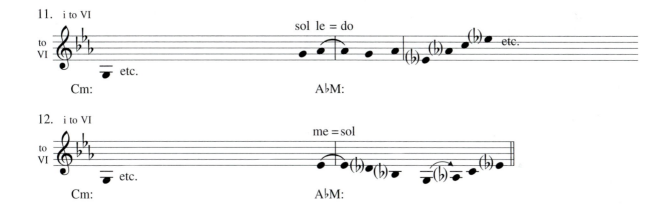

sol le = do

Cm: A♭M:

12. i to VI

me = sol

Cm: A♭M:

Modulatory patterns from C minor to B-flat major

13. i to VII

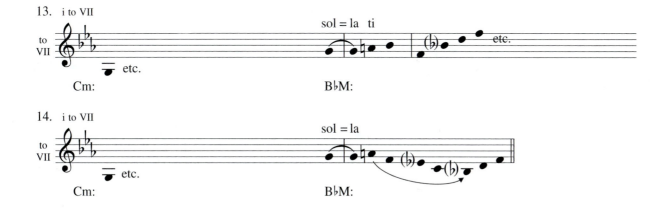

sol = la ti

Cm: B♭M:

14. i to VII

sol = la

Cm: B♭M:

15.

Bach *Ich freue mich* (I Am Glad), BWV 465 (tonicizations of V, VII, and III)

16.

Bach *Jesu, meines Glaubens* (Jesus, Ornament of My Faith), BWV 472 (tonicizations of V and ii)

17.

Bach *Wo ist mein Schäflein das ich liebe* (Where Is My Lamb which I Love), BWV 507 (tonicizations of V, vi, iii)

Using numbers 15, 16, and 17 as models, you are now invited to improvise three melodies.

C Melodies with Chromatic Alterations

This section contains 12 melodies by the Schumanns. Numbers 1–6 are by Clara Schumann; numbers 7–12 are by Robert Schumann.

The first three melodies are excerpts from Clara Schumann's Three songs, opus 12 (text by F. Rückert) [attributed to Clara Schumann within Robert Schumann's Liebesfrühling ("Spring of Love," op. 37, nos. 2, 4, 11)].

1.

Clara Schumann *Er ist gekommen in Sturm und Regen* (Through Storm and Tempest), op. 12, no. 2 (transposed)

2.

Clara Schumann *Liebst du um Schönheit* (Love You but Beauty), op. 12, no. 4 (transposed)

3.

Clara Schumann *Warum willst du andre fragen?* (Why Inquire of Other People?), op. 12, no. 11 (transposed)

Melodies 1–3 © 1990 by Breitkopf & Härtel, Wiesbaden.

Here are two other settings by Clara Schumann.

4.

Clara Schumann *Ich hab' in deinem Auge* (I Saw in Your Eyes), op. 13, no. 5 (abridged) (text also by Rückert) (transposed)

Clara Schumann *Was weinst du, Blümlein* (Why Are You Weeping, Little Flower), op. 23, no. 1 (abridged) (text by Rollett) (transposed)

5.

Melodies 4–5 © 1990 by Breitkopf & Härtel, Wiesbaden.

Clara Schumann Piano Trio (mm. 265–275)

6.

Breitkopf & Härtel, Wiesbaden. Used by permission.

Robert Schumann *Widmung* (Dedication), op. 25, no. 1 (transposed)

7.

8.

Sehr langsam

9.

Etwas kokett

10.

Langsam

11. **Sehr langsam** Robert Schumann *Stille Thränen* (Joy Comes), op. 35, no. 10

Robert Schumann *Nichts Schöneres* (Nothing More Beautiful), op. 36, no. 3 (transposed) (abridged)

12. **Einfach, innig**

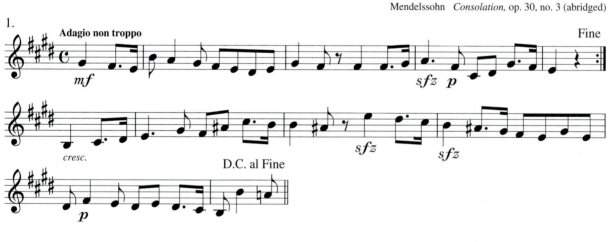

D Melodies with Chromatic Alterations: Modulating

All the melodies in this section are taken from works by Felix Mendelssohn (*Songs Without Words*). All include alterations due to one or another of the following: (a) accompaniments with secondary-dominant or leading-tone harmonies; (b) accompaniments with other chromatic harmonies such as borrowed chords, augmented 6ths, Neapolitan 6ths, and so on; (c) fully established modulations; and (d) chromatic nonharmonic tones. Your instructor will provide directions for the use of syllables or numbers as they relate to the sources of alteration listed above.

Mendelssohn *Consolation,* op. 30, no. 3 (abridged)

1.

Mendelssohn *Venetian Gondola Song,* op. 30, no. 6 (abridged) (transposed)

2.

3. **Allegro non troppo**

Mendelssohn *The Fleecy Cloud,* op. 53, no. 2 (abridged) (transposed)

4.

Mendelssohn *Sadness of Soul,* op. 53, no. 4 (abridged)

Adagio cantabile

5.

Mendelssohn *May Breezes,* op. 62, no. 1 (abridged) (transposed)

Andante espressivo

Mendelssohn *Spring Song,* op. 62, no. 6 (adapted and abridged)

6. **Allegretto grazioso**

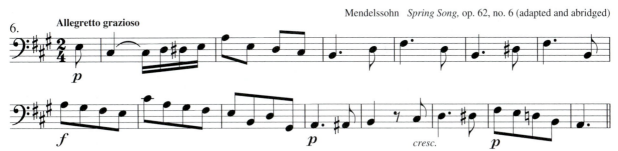

7.

Mendelssohn *Elegy,* op. 85, no. 4 (abridged) (transposed)

Andante sostenuto

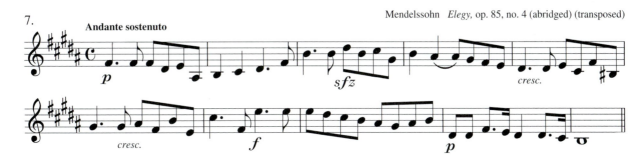

8.   Mendelssohn *Retrospection,* op. 102, no. 2 (abridged) (transposed)

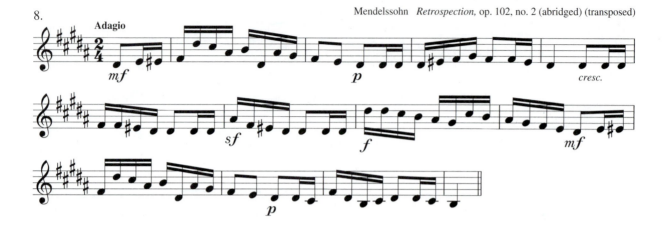

9.   Mendelssohn *Tarantella,* op. 102, no. 3 (abridged) (transposed)

Fine

D.C. al Fine

10.   Mendelssohn *Belief,* op. 102, no. 6 (abridged)

E Ensembles

SECTION 1. Ensemble Singing in Familiar Clefs

Beethoven *Freundschaft* (Friendship), Canon for Three Voices, WoO 164

G. P. Telemann *Fuga 2* (Fugue)

SECTION 2. Ensemble Singing in an Unfamiliar Clef

Haydn's *Thy Voice O Harmony* is a *cancrizans canon* in three voices—also known as a "crab canon"—also known as a retrograde canon. Can you find which line or lines sing the melody backward?

Haydn   *Thy Voice O Harmony*

Joseph Haydn Werke XXXI, Weltlichen Kanons, no. 46. © 1959 by G. Henle Verlag, Muenchen, used by permission.

UNIT ELEVEN

A   Rhythm—Compound Meter and Simple Meter: Irregular Divisions of the Beat (the Quartolet in Compound Meter, and the Triplet in Simple Meter)

SECTION 1.   Modules in Compound Meter and Simple Meter

Begin by repeating each module several times. Then treat the successive modules as a continuous exercise. Modules 1–40 are in compound meter; modules 41–48 are in simple meter.

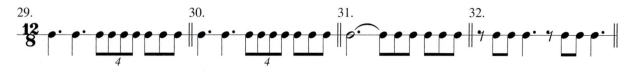

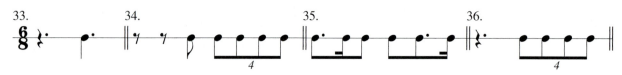

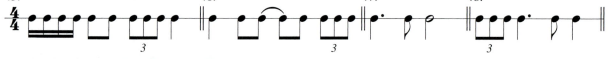

SECTION 2. Phrases in Compound Meter and Simple Meter with Irregular Divisions of the Beat

3.

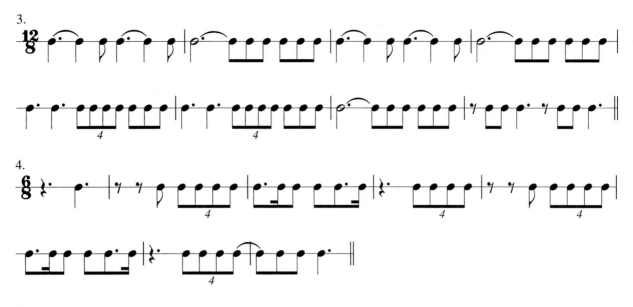

4.

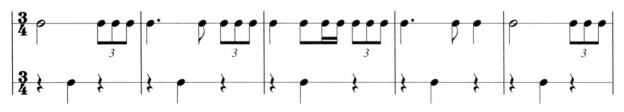

5. Rhythmic ostinato

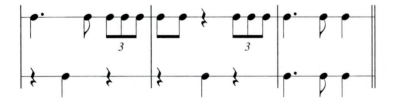

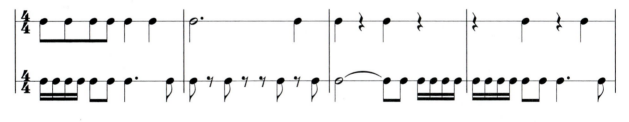

6. Upper rhythm repeated twice in lower voice in diminution

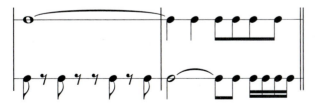

SECTION 3. Creating Coherent Phrases in Compound Meter and Simple Meter

Return to section 1 and select three or four rhythm modules, first in compound meter and then in simple meter. Place the modules in two coherent four-measure phrases, one in compound meter and the other in simple meter.

Write your solutions on the following lines:

Compound meter:

Simple meter:

B Diatonic and Chromatic Models and Melodic Fragments for Interval Study— New Intervals: d7 and A2

SECTION 1. Diatonic and Chromatic Models

The models in this section emphasize intervals of the diminished 7th (d7) and the augmented 2nd (A2).

The exercises in this section are in G♯ minor and relate to the music of Bach, Haydn, Beethoven, and Wagner. The models in this section relate to the fragments in the next section as follows:

Models	Fragments
1	1
2	2
3	3, 4, 5, 6
4	5
5	7a,b,c,d
6	7a,b,c,d
7	7a,b,c,d
8a	8
8b	8
9	11, 12, 13, 14
10	11, 12, 13, 14, 15

MODELS 1–4

All the d7s in these models extend from F𝄪 up to E or from E down to F𝄪.

Follow the same procedures as in previous units. For extra practice, sing the first model in all minor keys, transposing to each new key by P5s down or P4s up (see model below). Because the d7 is so neatly framed by the tonic triad, these patterns are excellent for "tossing," i.e., for singing in alternation between two groups, as in previous units.

MODELS 5–7

Models 5–7 outline the basic motives of the opening notes of Beethoven's Quartet op. 133 (The Grand Fugue). Melodic fragments 7a, b, c, and d are from the same quartet. Memorize model 7 so you can "hear" these fragments with your eyes when you reach section 2.

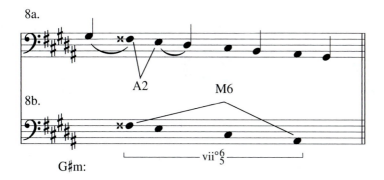

MODELS 8a AND 8b

These models focus on the A2 (from Fx down to E or from E up to Fx) representing the inversion of the d7. These A2s have the same pitches as the d7s in models 1–4. The leading-tone 7th chord in first inversion (vii°$_5^6$) is indicated in 8b and emphasizes the symmetry of the d7 chord.

8a.

8b.

MODELS 9–10

The leading-tone 7th chord, in root position, outlines the d7 chord and emphasizes the resulting symmetry (m3s or their enharmonic equivalent).

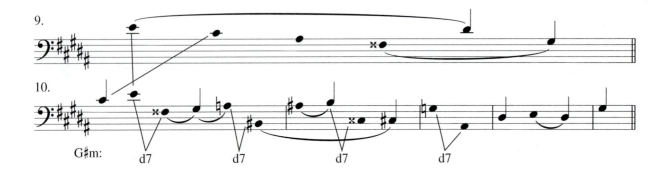

9.

10.

G♯m: d7   d7   d7   d7

SECTION 2. Melodic Fragments in G♯ Minor

Bach *Musikalisches Opfer* (The Musical Offering) (transposed)

1.

Lento

d7

2.
Beethoven   String Quartet op. 132, I

Assai sostenuto

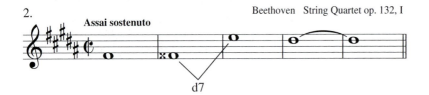

d7

3.
Beethoven   String Quartet op. 133, I (transposed)

Allegro molto e con brio

d7

4.
Bach   Two-Part Invention no. 4 (transposed)

Andante

d7   d7

5.
Bach   Three-Part Invention no. 2 (transposed)

Andante

d7   d7

6.
Bach   Two-Part Invention no. 2 (transposed)

Moderato

d7

7a.

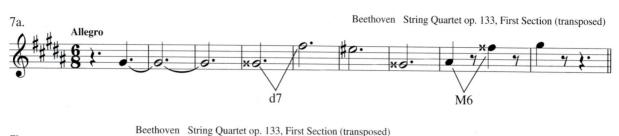

Beethoven   String Quartet op. 133, First Section (transposed)

7b.

Beethoven   String Quartet op. 133, First Section (transposed)

7c.

Beethoven   String Quartet op. 133, First Section (transposed)

7d.

Beethoven   String Quartet op. 133, First Section (transposed)

8.

Haydn   Piano Sonata XVI: 16 (transposed)

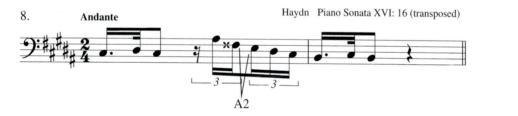

9.

Haydn   Piano Sonata XVI: 12 II (transposed)

10.

Haydn   Song *Dir nah ich mich, nah mich dem Throne* (I Approach You, I Approach the Throne) (transposed)

11.
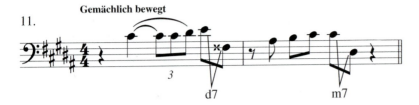

12.

13.

14.

15.

SECTION 3. Creating a Coherent Melody

Return to section 2 and select two or three segments of melodic fragments that create a coherent melody. It may be necessary to change the meter and rhythm of certain segments depending on your choice.

SECTION 4. Improvisation

The following parodies should help you to differentiate between minor-type modes (dorian, aeolian, and phrygian) and major-type modes (mixolydian, ionian, and lydian). Try to memorize these parodies so that you will be able to identify the characteristic intervallic patterns for each of the modes.

Minor-type parodies

1. Dorian

2. Aeolian

3. Phrygian

Major-type parodies

4. Mixolydian

5. Ionian

6. Lydian

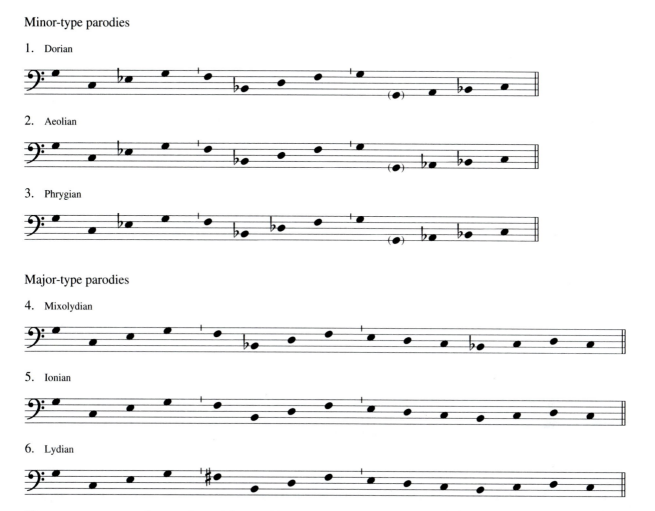

The next two songs are by trouvères of the twelfth and thirteenth centuries. The first is attributed to Colin Muset, who flourished from 1200–1250. The second is by Gace Brulé (1160–1213). (For additional examples from the same collection, see unit 6-C-songs 7–12.) These melodies are taken from the 1927 edition published by the University of Pennsylvania Press (printed in U.S.A. 1964), vol. II, titled *L'Édition du Corpus Cantilenarum Medii Aevi*. The numbers that appear together with each song are those of the 1927 (1964 printing) edition.

Use these melodies as models for modal improvisations.

Attributed to Colin Muset *Chanson* (Song), no. 108

1. ♩ = 60

Chanson (Song), no. 108 from *Les Chansonniers des Troubadours et des Trouvéres,* vol. 2, 1927. Reprinted by permission of the University of Pennsylvania Press.

2.   Gace Brulé *Reverdie,* no. 5

Chanson (Song), no. 5 from *Les Chansonniers des Troubadours et des Trouvéres,* vol. 2, 1927. Reprinted by permission of the University of Pennsylvania Press.

C Melodies with Unusual Modal Characteristics

These melodies are from various countries, including Russia, Ireland, Ethiopia, the former Czechoslovakia, and France. Some of these melodies are taken directly from the folk song literature. Others represent settings by composers such as Igor Stravinsky and Samuel Barber. The Stravinsky settings were written in Morges, Switzerland. C. F. Ramuz translated the Russian words into French. The song by Samuel Barber is based on a poem in French by Rainer Maria Rilke. Although the texts of these songs are not given in this unit, you are encouraged to seek out the modern settings of these works by studying scores in your library.

1.   Stravinsky *Timlimbom* from *Histoire pour enfants* (Three Tales for Children), no. 1 (abridged)

Timlimbom from *Histoire pour enfants* (Three Tales for Children), no. 1. Masters Music Publications, Inc., Publisher in the U.S.A.

"The Precious Treasure" from *Songs of the Irish*

2. **Allegretto**

From *Songs of the Irish* by Donal O'Sullivan. Published by Mercier Press, Cork, Ireland. Used by permission.

"Derreen Day" from *Songs of the Irish*

3. **Andante**

From *Songs of the Irish* by Donal O'Sullivan. Published by Mercier Press, Cork, Ireland. Used by permission.

The *Vocalise étude* by Gabriel Fauré is without text.

Fauré   *Vocalise étude*

4. **Adagio molto tranquillo**

Bohuslav Martinů *Fleur du Pecher* (Flower of the Peach Tree) (abridged)

5.

Samuel Barber *Le clocher chante* (The Bell Tower Sings), from *Mélodies passàgeres* (Transitory Melodies), op. 27, no. 4

6.

7. Stravinsky *Chanson pour compter* (Counting Song), from *Quatre Chants Russes* (Four Russian Songs), no. 2 (abridged)

8. Stravinsky *Canarde* (The Drake) *Ronde* from *Quatre Chants Russes* (Four Russian Songs), no. 1 (abridged)

Canarde Ronde by Igor Stravinsky. Masters Music Publications, Inc. Published in the U.S.A.

"Farewell to Carraig An Éide" from *Songs of the Irish*

9. **Poco pesante**

From *Songs of the Irish* by Donal O'Sullivan. Published by Mercier Press, Cork, Ireland. Used by permission.

10.

D Melodies—Chromatic Alterations: Modulating and Nonmodulating

SECTION 1. Sacred Melodies from Various Sources

All these melodies are sacred and include two Hebraic vocalises (Iordansky), a Negro spiritual ("Deep River"), an excerpt from Berlioz's *Te Deum*, and two examples of Gregorian Chant (Hymn to St. Thomas Aquinas, *In Paradisum*, from the Requiem Mass). The last four examples are from the *Complete Collection of Irish Music* by George Petrie (1789–1866), edited by Charles Villiers Stanford (1902): The Hymn of St. Bernard, The Funeral Cry (Galway, 1840), a Christmas Hymn (Galway), and an Irish Hymn (Londonderry).

Iordansky *Deux mélodies hébraïques* (Two Hebraic Melodies), 1

1. **Moderato**

2.   Iordansky   *Deux mélodies hébraïques* (Two Hebraic Melodies), 2

3.   "Deep River"   Negro Spiritual

4.   Berlioz   *Dignare Domine* (Prayer), *Te Deum*

5.   Hymn to St. Thomas Aquinas   Gregorian Chant

6.   In Paradisum (Into Paradise)   Gregorian Chant

7.   Jesu dulcis memoria (The Hymn of St. Bernard)   from Mr. Southwell

8.   Agitato   Funeral Cry   Galway, August 28th, 1840

9.   Lento (♩ = 69)   Christmas Carol or Hymn (as sung in the county of Galway)   from Mrs. Close

10.

Andante

Irish Hymn Sung on the Dedication of a Chapel, Co. of Londonderry

SECTION 2. Songs by Brahms

All the following melodies are excerpts from songs by Brahms.

1.
Sehr lebhaft

Brahms *Tambourliedchen* (The Little Drummer's Song), op. 69, no. 5 (abridged and transposed)

2.
Etwas bewegt

Brahms *Therese,* op. 86, no. 1 (abridged)

3. Bewegt und heimlich

Brahms *Spannung* (Tension), op. 84, no. 5 (abridged and transposed)

4. **Andante moderato**

Brahms *Anklänge* (Reminiscences), op. 7, no. 3 (abridged)

p

Brahms *So willst du des Armen dich gnädig erbarmen?* ('Tis Not Then a Dream?), from *Romanzen aus Magelone* (Romances from Magelone), op. 33, no. 5 (abridged and transposed)

5. **Allegro**

Brahms *Über die Heide* (Over the Heath), op. 86, no. 4 (abridged)

6. **Ziemlich langsam, gehend**

Brahms *Der Jäger* (The Huntsman), op. 95, no. 4 (abridged and transposed)

7. **Lebhaft**

Brahms *Trennung* (Separation), op. 97, no. 6 (abridged and transposed)

8. **Anmutig bewegt**

Brahms *An den Mond* (To the Moon), op. 71, no. 2 (abridged)

9. **Nicht zu langsam und mit Anmut**

10.

Brahms *Spanisches Lied* (Spanish Song), op. 6, no. 1 (abridged)

E Ensembles

SECTION 1. Ensemble Singing in Familiar Clefs

1.

Brahms Thirteen Canons op. 113, 1 *Göttlicher Morpheus* (Divine Morpheus) (Text: Goethe)

Printed with the friendly permission of Breitkopf & Härtel, Wiesbaden.

Brahms   Thirteen Canons op. 113, 2 *Grausam erweiset sich Amor an mir* (Amor Proves to Be So Cruel) (Text: Goethe)

Printed with the friendly permission of Breitkopf & Härtel, Wiesbaden.

Brahms   Thirteen Canons, op. 113, 3 *Sitzt a schöns Vögerl aufm Dannabaum* (There Sits a Lovely Bird upon the Christmas Tree)
(Text: traditional Austrian in A. von Kretzschmer and A.W. von Zuccalmaglio: German folksong)

3.

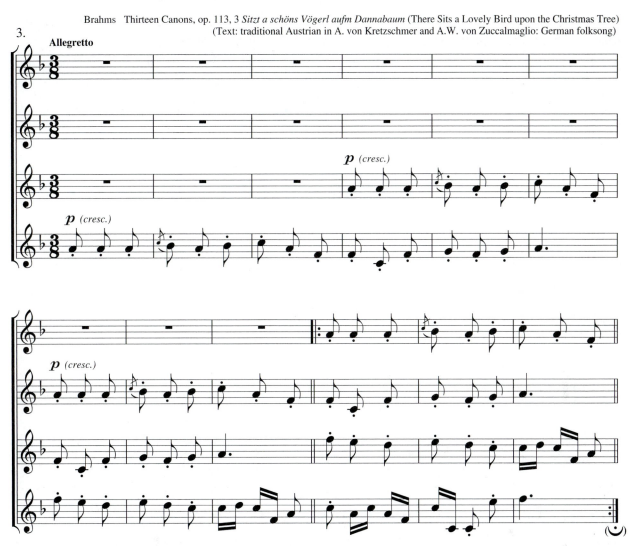

Printed with the friendly permission of Breitkopf & Härtel, Wiesbaden.

The Bb clarinet sounds a M2 lower than written. Use the tenor clef to indicate c" in singing the transposition. Check
your accuracy in the reading of the clarinet part with the harp part. Both lines sound in unison.

Mahler *Der Abschied* (The Farewell), from *Das Lied von der Erde* (Song of the Earth)

Die Blu - men blass - en   im Däm - mer - schein.

SECTION 2. Ensemble Singing in Unfamiliar Clefs

Here we have the canon without realization (realization is found in subsequent example). In the dedication copy, Bach added the note, "Ascendenteque Modulatione ascendat Gloria Regis" (And may the glory of the King rise with the rising modulation); quoted from the Dover edition.

Bach *Musikalisches Opfer* (The Musical Offering)

Bach *The Musical Offering*, Canon no. 5 *Per tonos*∗ realization by J. P. Kirnberger; translated as (Ascending through the keys) in the Dover edition.

Bach *Musikalisches Opfer* (The Musical Offering)

2.

UNIT TWELVE

A Rhythm—Compound Meter and Simple Meter: Subdivisions of the Beat into Eight Parts

SECTION 1. Modules in Compound Meter and Simple Meter

Begin by repeating each module several times. Then treat the successive modules as a continuous exercise.

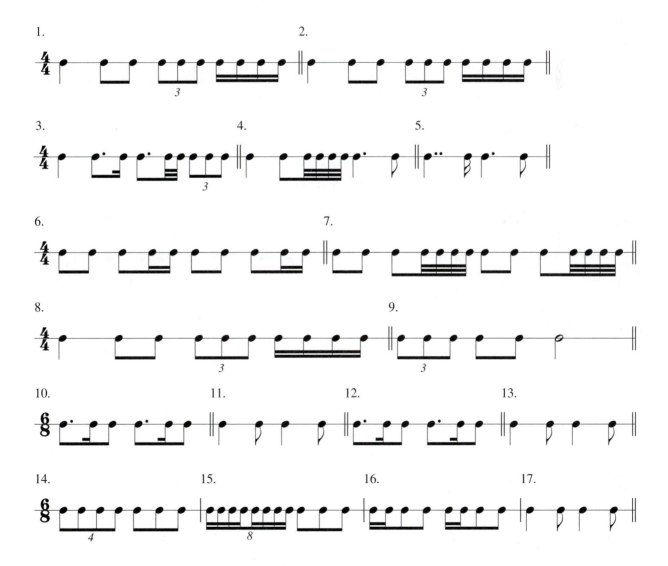

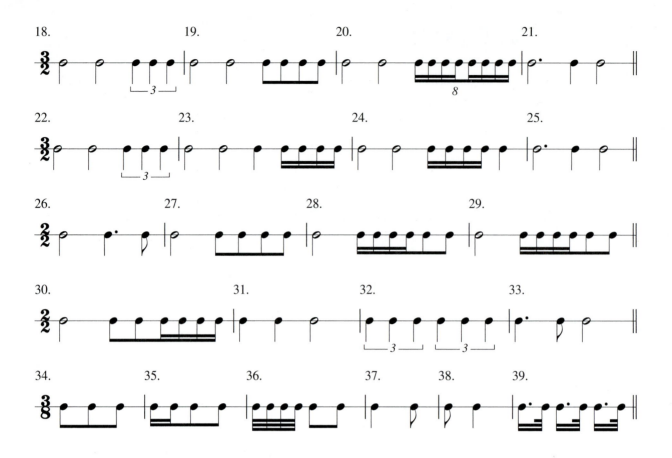

SECTION 2. Phrases in Compound Meter and Simple Meter with Subdivisions of the Beat into Eight Parts

SECTION 3. Creating Coherent Phrases in Compound Meter and Simple Meter

Return to section 1 and select three or four rhythm modules, first in compound meter and then in simple meter. Place the modules in two coherent four-measure phrases, one in compound meter and the other in simple meter.

Write your solutions on the following lines:

Compound meter:

Simple meter:

B Diatonic and Chromatic Models and Melodic Fragments for Interval Study— New Intervals: A6 and d3

SECTION 1. Diatonic and Chromatic Models

The models in this section emphasize intervals of the augmented 6th (A6) and the diminished 3rd (d3).

The exercises in this section are in B minor or B major and relate to the music of Beethoven and Mozart. When you reach the next section, you will notice that a bass line is provided for most of the fragments to show voice-leading principles involving the augmented 6th (A6) and its resolution to an octave (on the dominant). Implied harmonies are also provided.

The models in this section relate to the fragments of the next section as follows:

Models	Fragments
1, 2, 3, 4	1, 2, 3, 4
5, 6	5, 6*
7, 8, 9	8, 9, 10

* The model for fragment 7 appears as 7a in section 2.

MODELS 1–4

These models follow the contour of the A6 chord, outlining each factor.

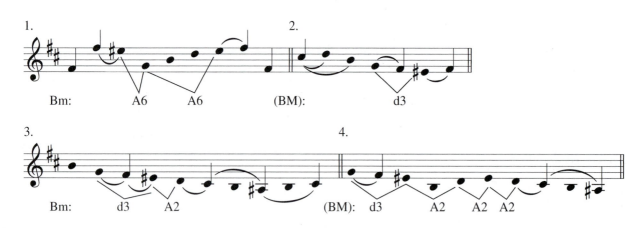

MODELS 5–6

If the implications of A6 chords are not apparent in these exercises, they will become more evident in the melodic fragments (section D), where a second voice is added.

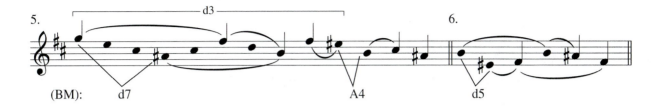

MODELS 7–9

These exercises show how the A6 chord might be used as a pivot chord in modulations. For additional practice, repeat these patterns in various keys in an attempt to out-modulate both Beethoven and Mozart.

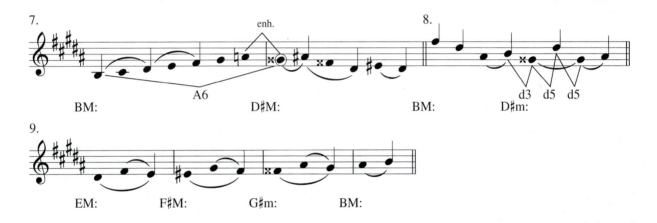

SECTION 2. Melodic Fragments in B Minor and B Major

MELODIC FRAGMENTS FOR INTERVAL STUDY—NEW INTERVALS: A6 AND d3

2. Mozart *La finta giardiniera* (Opera) (The Girl in Gardener's Disguise) (transposed)

BM: Gr6   V

Mozart   Recitative from *Les noces de Figaro* (The Marriage of Figaro)

3.

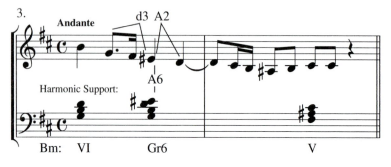

Bm: VI   Gr6   V

Mozart *La Clemenza di Tito* (Titus's Clemency) (transposed) (abridged)

4.

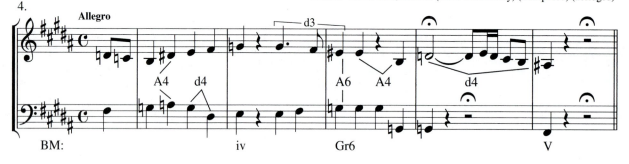

BM: iv   Gr6   V

Mozart *La Clemenza di Tito* (Titus's Clemency) (transposed) (abridged)

5.

BM: iv   I   iv   V   i   Fr6   V

Mozart *Les noces de Figaro* (The Marriage of Figaro) (transposed)

6.

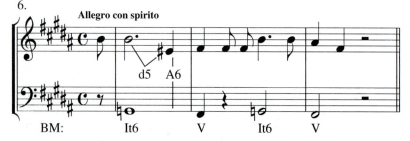

BM: It6   V   It6   V

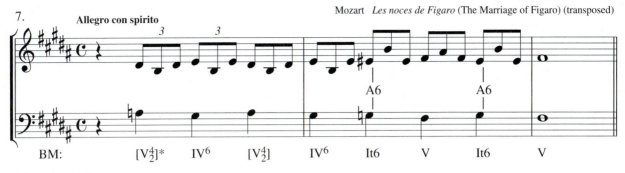

7. **Allegro con spirito**

Mozart *Les noces de Figaro* (The Marriage of Figaro) (transposed)

BM: [V$^4_2$]*   IV^6 [V$^4_2$]   IV^6 It6   V   It6   V

* Secondary dominant

7a.   Reduction of no. 7

BM:

8.

Beethoven   Symphony no. 5, op. 67, II (transposed)

Andante con moto

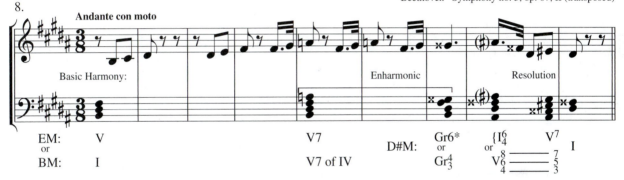

EM: V

or

BM: I

V7

V7 of IV

D#M: Gr6*

or

Gr$^4_3$

{I$^6_4$ V^7

or

V$^8_6$$_4$ — $^7_5$$_3$ I

* Functions as doubly A4

9.   **Allegro agitato**

Mozart *La finta giardiniera* (Opera) (The Girl in Gardener's Disguise) (transposed)

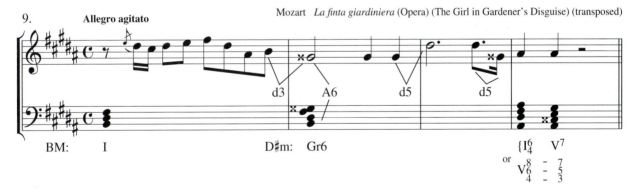

BM: I

D♯m: Gr6

{I$^6_4$ V^7

or

V$^8_6$$_4$ – $^7_5$$_3$

10.

Mozart *Die Entführung aus dem Serail* (Opera) (The Abduction from the Seraglio) (transposed)

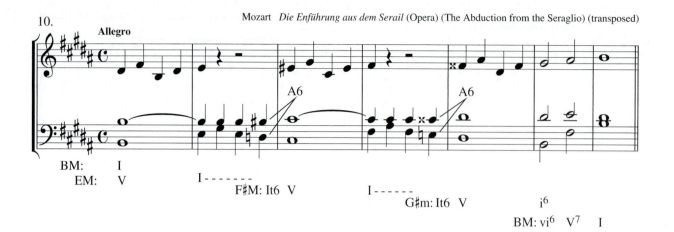

Supplemental fragments to show voice-leading principles involving the diminished third (G♮–E♯) brought about by the motion of the lowered second scale degree (G♮) to the leading tone (E♯ and tonic (F♯).

Beethoven   Variations on "God Save the King," WoO 78 (Var. 5, m. 5—transposed from C minor)

11.

Purcell   *King Arthur* (Frost Scene)—Cold Genius (transposed from C minor)

12.

SECTION 3.   Creating a Coherent Melody

Return to section 2 and select two or three segments of melodic fragments that would create a coherent melody. It may be necessary to change the meter and rhythm of certain segments, depending on your choice.

SECTION 4. Improvisation

Once again, we are returning to the vocalise pattern of Unit 7, B-4. By extending this pattern, it will be possible to reinterpret V^7 in the original key as a German augmented sixth chord in a new key that is a minor second lower than the original key. This extended vocalise pattern can be modified to give practice in using the Italian augmented sixth chord and the French augmented sixth chord in modulatory patterns.

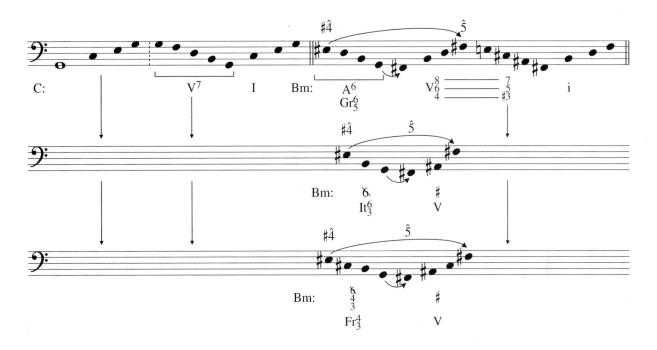

Use this fragment in C major from Bellini's *Come per me sereno* (How Peacefully for Me) from his opera *La Sonnambula* as an extended vocalise pattern to reinterpret the V^7 as a German augmented sixth chord so that you can modulate to B minor. Improvise a new vocalise in B minor and move through the minor keys in descending motion: from B minor to B-flat minor and so on.

Bellini   *Come per me sereno* (How peacefully for me), from *La Sonnambula* (The Sleepwalker)

Adapted from *Come per me sereno* by Vincenzo Bellini, and published in *Embellished Opera Arias,* edited by Austin B. Caswell. Recent Researches in the Music of the Nineteenth and Early Twentieth Centuries, vols. 7–8. Madison, Wisconsin: A-R Editions, Inc. 1989. Used with permission.

Return to the improvisation patterns that you created in unit 7-B-4, based on fragments from Mozart's The Magic Flute and centered around the dominant 7th, and move through minor keys in descending motion.

C Melodies with Unusual Modal Characteristics

As with the melodies in unit 11, part C, some of these melodies are from various countries, including Bulgaria, Greece, Ireland, Russia, Spain, and the United States. Other examples represent a setting by Mussorgsky, vocalises by Kodaly and Milhaud, examples of twelfth century chant by Hildegard von Bingen, the traditional "Dies Irae" from Gregorian chant, and a setting of the same text as sung in the county of Londonderry. Some of these melodies illustrate melodic patterns that are characteristic of modes such as dorian, phrygian, lydian, mixolydian, and aeolian and combinations of one or more of these modes; other patterns have unusual modal qualities that are not indicative of the church modes.

1. *Dies Irae* (Day of Wrath) Gregorian chant (*Mass for the Dead*) Dorian mode

2. *Dies Irae* (Day of Wrath)—as sung in the Co. of Londonderry

3. "A Bold Child" (Ionian mode)   Ireland

From *Songs of the Irish* by Donal O'Sullivan. Published by Mercier Press, Cork, Ireland. Used by permission.

4.   "Barbara Ellen" (Pentatonic)

BARBARA ELLEN from *80 Appalachian Folk Songs* collected by Cecil Sharp & Maude Karpeles. © Copyright 1968 by Faber Music, Ltd., London. Copyright Renewed. Reprinted by kind permission of Faber Music Ltd., London.

5.   Folk song   Greece (Dorian mode)

6.   Milhaud   *Vocalise Étude*

Reproduced with amiable authorization from Editions Alphonse Leduc-Paris.

7.   Stravinsky   *Berceuse* (Aeolian mode)

Berceuse (Aeolian mode), Igor Stravinsky; Robert Craft. *Expositions and Developments.* Reprinted by permission of the University of California Press, Berkeley, California.

8.   Hildegard von Bingen   *The Ursula Antiphons,* 5. *Deus Enim* (God Certainly) (Phrygian) (transcribed and edited by Pozzi Escot)

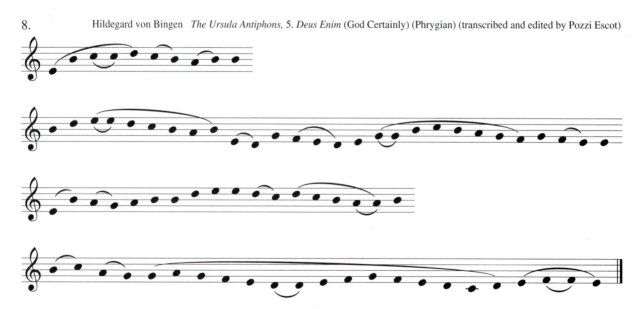

Deus enim, #5 from *The Nine Ursula Antiphons* by Hildegard von Bingen, transcribed and edited by Pozzi Escot. Reprinted with permission of Publication Contact International, Cambridge, MA.

9. Hildegard von Bingen *The Ursula Antiphons, 6. Aer Enim* (Air Certainly) (Phrygian) (transcribed and edited by Pozzi Escot)

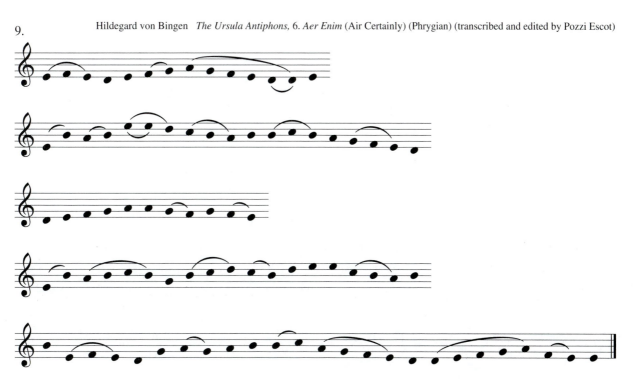

Aer enim, #8 from *The Nine Ursula Antiphons* by Hildegard von Bingen, transcribed and edited by Pozzi Escot. Reprinted with permission of Publication Contact International, Cambridge, MA.

10. "The Lone Rock" (Folk song) (Aeolian mode)   Ireland

Andante

From *Songs of the Irish* by Donal O'Sullivan. Published by Mercier Press, Cork, Ireland. Used by permission.

11. "Young Lad" (Folk song) (Ionian mode)   Ireland

Andantino

From *Songs of the Irish* by Donal O'Sullivan. Published by Mercier Press, Cork, Ireland. Used by permission.

12.

Mussorgsky   *Boris Godunov,* "Polonaise" (Lydian mode)

Alla polacca

13. **Non troppo allegro**

"The Fair Hills of E'ire O!" (Mixolydian mode)   Irish folk song

14.

Poco sostenuto

From *Songs of the Irish* by Donal O'Sullivan. Published by Mercier Press, Cork, Ireland. Used by permission.

15. **Appassionato**

From *Songs of the Irish* by Donal O'Sullivan. Published by Mercier Press, Cork, Ireland. Used by permission.

Bulgarian folk song   (Modal mixture)

16. **Allegro**

17. Kodály   *Epigrams* (Nine Vocalises), 1

Lento

18. **Allegretto con semplicità**

* A Chippewa Indian theme collected by Frances Densmore

Navalafuente Spanish

19. **Villancico** ♩ = 116

Cancionero Popular de la Provincia de Madrid Volume III, collected by Manuel Garcia Matos, critical edition by Juán Tomás Parés & José Romeu Figureas. Instituto Espanol de Musicología, Barcelona–Madrid 1960.

"The Blackthorn Tree"   Irish folk song

20. **Affettuoso**

From *Songs of the Irish* by Donal O'Sullivan. Published by Mercier Press, Cork, Ireland. Used by permission.

D Melodies—Chromatic Alterations: Modulating and Nonmodulating

SECTION 1. Melodies by Schubert

All the melodies in this section contain modulations.

Schubert *Wasserflut* (Flood of Tears), from *Winterreise* (Winter Journey), D. 911, no. 6

1. **Langsam**

Schubert *Rückblick* (Glance Back), from *Winterreise* (Winter Journey), D. 911, no. 8

2. **Nicht zu geschwind**

Schubert *Rast* (Rest), from *Winterreise* (Winter Journey), D. 911, no. 10

3. **Mässig**

Schubert *Einsamkeit* (Solitude), from *Winterreise* (Winter Journey), D. 911, no. 12

4.

Schubert *Die Post* (The Mail Coach), from *Winterreise* (Winter Journey), D. 911, no. 13

5.

Schubert *Im Dorfe* (In the Village), from *Winterreise* (Winter Journey), D. 911, no. 17

6. **Etwas langsam**

Schubert *Der Stürmische* (The Stormy Morning), from *Winterreise* (Winter Journey), D. 911, no. 18

7. **Ziemlich geschwind, doch dräftig**

Schubert *Täuschung* (Deception), from *Winterreise* (Winter Journey), D. 911, no. 19

8. **Etwas geschwind**

Schubert *Das Wirtshaus* (The Inn), from *Winterreise* (Winter Journey), D. 911, no. 21

9. **Sehr langsam**

Schubert *Die böse Farbe* (The Evil Color), from *Die schöne Müllerin* (The Fair Miller Maid), D. 795, no. 17

10. **Ziemlich geschwind**

SECTION 2. Clef Reading and Transposition

Melodies in this section are from songs by Gustav Mahler and Fanny Mendelssohn Hensel (sister of Felix Mendelssohn).

Transpose this melody down a m3 by thinking in soprano clef. Substitute the A major key signature. The starting note is a (the a' above middle C).

Gustav Mahler *Das Trinklied vom Jammer der Erde* (The Drinking Song of the Earth's Lament), from *Das Lied von der Erde* (The Song of the Earth)

1. **Allegro pesante with vigor**

Transpose this melody down a m3 by thinking in soprano clef. Substitute the D major key signature for lines 1 and 2 and G major for lines 3 and 4. The starting note for each excerpt is:

Excerpt W: d" (octave and a 2nd above middle C)
Excerpt X: g' (above middle C)
Excerpt Y: c" (above middle C)

Gustav Mahler *Der Einsame im Herbst* (The Lonely One in Autumn), from *Das Lied von der Erde* (The Song of the Earth)

Gustav Mahler *Von der Jugend* (Of Youth), from *Das Lied von der Erde* (The Song of the Earth)

* The clarinet is in B♭. Transpose down a M2 by thinking in tenor clef. Substitute the B♭ major key signature.
The starting note is b♭' (above middle C, c').

Transpose down a m3 by thinking in soprano clef. Substitute the key signature for G. The starting note is d.'

Gustav Mahler *Von der Jugend* (Of Youth), from *Das Lied von der Erde* (The Song of the Earth)

Gustav Mahler *Nun will die Sonn' so hell aufgehn!* (Now the Sun Will Rise So Brightly),
from *Kinder-Totenlieder* (Songs on the Death of Children), no. 1

6.

Gemessen dumpf (nicht schleppen)
In time, resigned, without dragging

Gustav Mahler *Der Tamboursg'sell* (The Drummer Boy)

Gustav Mahler *Wenn mein Schatz Hochzeit* (My Sweetheart's Wedding Day),
from *Lieder eines fahrenden Gesellen* (Songs of a Wayfarer), no. 1

7.

Allegro

Gustav Mahler *Ging heut' Morgen über's Feld* (This Morning I Went through the Fields),
from *Lieder eines fahrenden Gesellen,* (Songs of a Wayfarer), no. 2

8.

Gemächlich

9.

Mahler *Das himmlische Leben* (The Heavenly Life) (abridged)

© 1993 by Universal Edition A. G., Wien/UE 19950.

10.

Fanny Mendelssohn Hensel *Schwanenlied* (Swansong)

Reprinted by permission of G. Schirmer, Inc. (ASCAP).

E Ensembles

SECTION 1. Ensemble Singing in Familiar Clefs

Brahms *Ich weiss* (I Wonder Why the Dove So Sad Is Cooing!), from *Thirteen Canons,* op. 113, no. 11; text by Rückert

Schubert *Liebe säuseln die Blätter* (The Leaves Rustle of Love), D988 (text from Hölty's *Maigesang*)

Lie - be säu - seln die Blät - ter, Lie - be duf - ten die Blü - then,

Lie - be säu - seln die Blät - ter, Lie - be duf - ten die Blü - then,

Lie - be rie - selt die Quel - le, Lie - be flö - tet die Nach - ti - gall.

Lie - be rie - selt die Quel - le, Lie - be flö - tet die Nach - ti - gall.

Lie - be säu - seln die Blät - ter, Lie - be duf - ten die Blü -

Lie - be säu - seln die Blät - ter, Lie - be duf - ten die Blü - then,

Lie - be säu - seln die Blät - ter, Lie - be duf - ten die Blü - then,

Lie - be säu-seln die Blät - ter, Lie - be duf - ten die Blü - then,

Lie - be säu-seln die Blät - ter, Lie - be duf - ten die Blü - then,

Lie - be säu - seln die Blät - ter, Lie - be duf - ten die Blü -

Lie-be rie-selt die Quel - le, Lie-be flö - tet die Nach - ti-gall.

Lie-be rie-selt die Quel - le, Lie-be flö - tet die Nach - ti-gall.

then, Lie - be rie - selt die Quel - le, Lie - be flö - tet die Nach-ti-gall.

3.
Schütz *Introitus* (Introit), from *Die sieben Worte Jesu Christi* (The Seven Last Words of Christ)

SECTION 2. Ensemble Singing in Unfamiliar Clefs

This chorale is from Cantata 103. The continuo line is provided for convenience. Students are encouraged to perform this work vocally and instrumentally.

Bach Chorale *Ich hab' dich einen Augenblick* (I Have Forsaken You Only for a Moment, Dear Child) Cantata 103

Printed with the friendly permission of Breitkopf & Härtel, Wiesbaden.

UNIT THIRTEEN

A Rhythm—Simple Meter: The Supertriplet

SECTION 1. Modules in Simple Meter

Begin by repeating each module several times. Then treat the successive modules as a continuous exercise.

SECTION 2. Phrases in Simple Meter with Supertriplets

SECTION 3. Creating a Coherent Phrase in Simple Meter with Supertriplets

Return to section 1 and select three or four rhythm modules. Place the modules into a coherent four-measure phrase.

Write your solution on the following line:

B Diatonic and Chromatic Models and Melodic Fragments for Interval Study—New Interval: d4

SECTION 1. Diatonic and Chromatic Models

The models in this section emphasize the diminished 4th (d4) and relate to the music of Ellington, Liszt, Bach, Beethoven, Haydn, and Schubert (see section 2). The models (exercises) of this section prefigure the fragments in the following manner:

Models	Fragments
1, 2	1, 2
3, 4	3, 4
5	5, 6, 7
6	5, 8
7	10
8	8, 10

For further practice, sing exercise 5 in all minor keys, transposing to each new key by P5 down or P4 up (see model below).

SECTION 2. Melodic Fragments in A♭ Major (F Minor)

A♭ major:

1.

Ellington "Mood Indigo"

Slowly

d4

MOOD INDIGO from SOPHISTICATED LADIES. Words and music by Duke Ellington, Irving Mills, and Albany Bigard. Copyright © 1931 (Renewed 1958) and Assigned to EMI Mills Music, Inc., Famous Music Corporation, and Indigo Mood Music c/o The Songwriters Guild of America in the U.S.A. Rights for the world outside the U.S.A. controlled by EMI Mills Music, Inc. (Publishing) and Alfred Publishing Co., Inc. (Print). International copyright secured. All rights reserved.

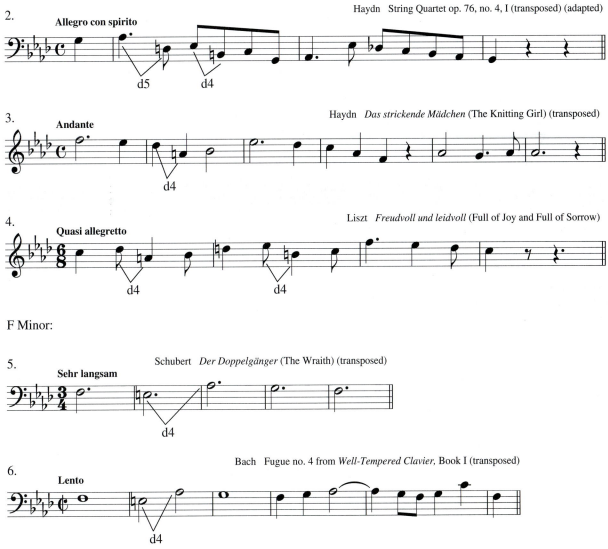

2.

Haydn   String Quartet op. 76, no. 4, I (transposed) (adapted)

Allegro con spirito

d5   d4

3.

Haydn   *Das strickende Mädchen* (The Knitting Girl) (transposed)

Andante

d4

4.

Liszt   *Freudvoll und leidvoll* (Full of Joy and Full of Sorrow)

Quasi allegretto

d4   d4

F Minor:

5.

Schubert   *Der Doppelgänger* (The Wraith) (transposed)

Sehr langsam

d4

6.

Bach   Fugue no. 4 from *Well-Tempered Clavier*, Book I (transposed)

Lento

d4

SECTION 3. Creating a Coherent Melody

Return to section 2 and select two or three segments of melodic fragments that create a coherent melody. It may be necessary to change the meter and rhythm of certain segments, depending on your choice.

SECTION 4. Improvisation

Use the first four measures of Duke Ellington's "Mood Indigo" (see melodic fragment 1) as the basis for an improvisation. In case you are wondering how the rest of the tune goes, look at melody 4 in section D of this unit. Use your improvisation as a backdrop for your own words or for the original text which is as follows:

*Mood Indigo**

You ain't been blue; no, no, no.
You ain't been blue,
Till you've had that mood indigo.
That feelin' goes stealin' down to my shoes
While I sit and sigh, "Go 'long blues."

Always get that mood indigo.
Since my baby said goodbye.
In the evenin' when lights are low,
I'm so lonesome I could cry.

'Cause there's nobody who cares about me,
I'm just a soul who's bluer than blue can be.
When I get that mood indigo,
I could lay me down and die.

C Melodies Related to Jazz

SECTION 1. The Blues Repertoire

These melodies are by composers such as Chris Smith, Perry Bradford, and Cab Calloway.

Chris Smith   "Ballin' the Jack"

2.

Chris Smith   "Boom, Tum, Ta-Ra-Ra—Zing Boom!"   Lyrics by Ferd. E. Mierisch

Boom, tum - ta - ra - ra   Zing Boom!

Boom, tum - ta - ra - ra   Zing Boom!

Boom, Tum, Ta-Ra - Ra   -   Zing Boom!

Boom tum-ta - ra - ra! Zing   Boom! Zing

3.

Perry Bradford "That Thing Called Love"

Moderato

Perry Bradford "Crazy Blues"

4.

5. **Moderato**

Chorus

Words by Mitch Parish, Music by Frank Perkins and Cab Calloway   "The Scat Song"

skat' n   skeet' n

hi - de hi - and skat-tle at - tle at da day __

skat' n   skeet' n   hi - de hi, __ and skat-tle at - tle at da day __

__

skat' n   skeet' n   hi - de hi, __ and skat-tle at - tle at   da day __

THE SCAT SONG Music by Frank Perkins and Cab Calloway. Words by Mitchell Parish. © EMI Mills Music, Inc. and Hi De Ho Man Music (c/o EMI Mills Music, Inc.). Worldwide rights administered by Alfred Publishing Co., Inc. All rights reserved.

SECTION 2. Vocalises by Alec Wilder

These five vocalises were written for Eileen Farrell by Alec Wilder in 1972. They represent an interesting blend of classical and jazz idioms.

Wilder *Vocalise 2*

FIVE VOCALISES FOR SOPRANO AND PIANO. By Alec Wilder. Copyright © 1947 (Renewed) by Associated Music Publishers, Inc. (BMI). International Copyright Secured. All Rights Reserved. Reprinted by Permission.

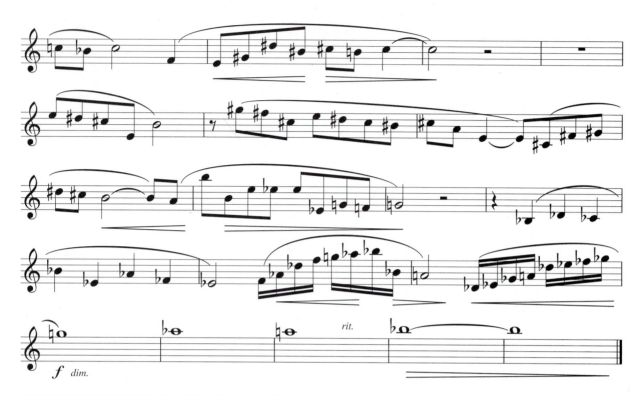

D Melodies by Duke Ellington

Chord changes for the Ellington melodies are given to inspire your keyboard harmonizations. Whenever possible, harmonize the melodies and accompany them as you sing.

Billy Strayhorn and the Delta Rhythm Boys   "Take the 'A' Train"

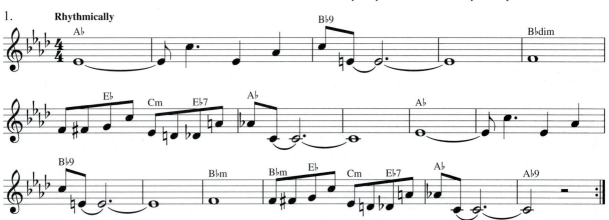

Duke Ellington, Irving Mills, and Rex Stewart   "Boy Meets Horn"

Duke Ellington, Eddie DeLange, and Irving Mills   "Solitude"

Duke Ellington, Irving Mills, and Albany Bigard "Mood Indigo"

4. **Slowly**

Duke Ellington, Irving Mills, and Manny Kurtz "In a Sentimental Mood"

5. **Slowly with expression**

Duke Ellington and Billy Strayhorn "Day Dream"

6. **Slow**

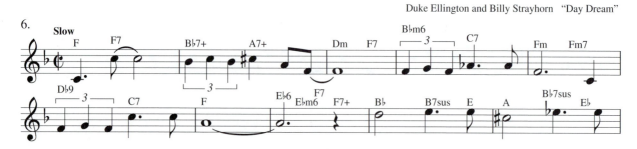

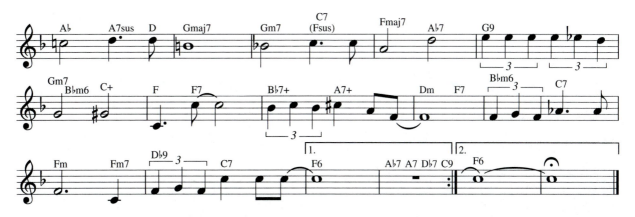

DAY DREAM Words by John La Touche, Music by Duke Ellington and Billy Strayhorn. Copyright © 1940, 1941; Renewed 1968, 1969 Dimensional Music Of 1091 (ASCAP), Billy Strayhorn Songs, Inc. (ASCAP), Famous Music Corporation (ASCAP) and EMI Robbins Catalog Inc. (ASCAP) for the U.S.A. and the British Reversionary Territories. Rights for Dimensional Music Of 1091 and Billy Strayhorn Songs, Inc. administered by Cherry Lane Music Publishing Company, Inc. Rights for the rest of the world controlled by EMI Robbins Catalog Inc. (Publishing) and Alfred Publishing Co., Inc. (Print) International copyright secured. All rights reserved.

Duke Ellington, Harry James, and Don George   "Everything but You"

7. **Moderate and rhythmic**

EVERYTHING BUT YOU by Duke Ellington, Harry James and Don George. Copyright © 1941 (Renewed) by Music Sales Corporation (ASCAP) and Tempo Music, Inc. (ASCAP). All Rights Administered by Music Sales Corporation (ASCAP). Copyright © 1945 (Renewed 1972) by Famous Music Corporation, Music Sales Corporation (ASCAP) and Publisher Unknown. International Copyright Secured. All Rights Reserved. Reprinted by Permission.

8. **Moderately**

Duke Ellington and Paul Webster   "I Got It Bad (And That Ain't Good)"
from the American Revue Theatre Production *Jump for Joy*

9. **Slowly**   Duke Ellington, Irving Mills, Henry Nemo, and John Redmond   "I Let a Song Go Out of My Heart"

Duke Ellington and Mack David   "I'm Just a Lucky So-and-So"

10. **Very slow**

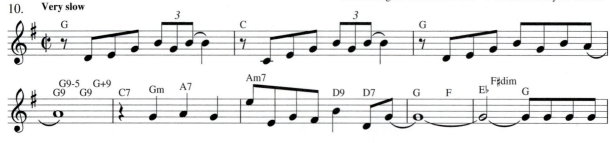

"I'm Just a Lucky So-and-So" Words by Mack David, Music by Duke Ellington. Copyright © 1945 (Renewed 1973) and assigned to Paramount Music Corp. and Universal-PolyGram International Publishing, Inc. in the U.S.A. Rights for the world outside the U.S.A. controlled by Paramount Music Corp. International Copyright Secured. All Rights Reserved.

E   Ensembles

SECTION 1.   Ensemble Singing in Familiar Clefs

James Weldon Johnson and R. Rosamond Johnson   "Lift Every Voice and Sing" (National Negro Hymn)

lis - t'ning _ skies, Let it re - sound loud as the roll - ing sea. ____
wea - ry _ feet Come to the place for which our fa - thers sighed? _
to the _ light, Keep us for - ev - er in the path, __ we pray. __

Sing a song full of the faith that the dark past has taught us,
We have come o - ver a way that with tears has been wa - tered,
Lest our feet stray from the pla - ces, our God, where we met Thee,

Sing a song full of the hope that the pres - ent has brought __
We have come, tread - ing our path thro' the blood of the slaugh -
Lest our hearts, drunk with the wine of the world, we for - get ____

ff

us; Fac - ing the ris - ing sun of our new day be -
tered, Out from the gloom - y past, till now we stand at ____
Thee; Sha - dowed be - neath Thy hand, may we for - ev - er ____

gun, Let us march on till vic - to - ry _____ is won.
last Where the white gleam of our bright star _____ is cast.
stand, True to our God, true to our na - tive land.

SECTION 2. Ensemble Singing in Unfamiliar Clefs

Just as in unit 11 E-2 where we had a puzzle canon from Bach's Musical Offering with Kirnberger's solution, here we have another intriguing example from the same work. In this case, the original melody (left to right) is designed to appear in retrograde (right to left) in the second part. This process is known as *cancrizans*.

1.   Bach *Musikalisches Opfer* (The Musical Offering), BWV 1079

2. Bach   Kirnberger

Here is a puzzle canon by Schoenberg, written in 1934. Notice how Schoenberg follows the same compositional technique as Bach in using the original theme in retrograde.

UNIT FOURTEEN

A Rhythm—Simple Meter and Compound Meter: The Subtriplet

SECTION 1. Modules in Simple Meter

Begin by repeating each module several times. Then treat the successive modules as a continuous exercise.

SECTION 2. Phrases in Simple Meter and Compound Meter with Subtriplets

6.

SECTION 3. Creating a Coherent Phrase in Simple Meter with Subtriplets

Return to section 1 and select three or four rhythm modules. Place the modules into a coherent four-measure phrase.

Write your solution on the following line:

B Diatonic, Chromatic, Whole-Tone, and Octatonic Models and Melodic Fragments for Interval Study

SECTION 1. Diatonic, Chromatic, Whole-Tone, and Octatonic Models

The models in this section emphasize modal mixture, enharmonic changes, motivic structure, chromatic, whole-tone, and octatonic fragments. The musical fragments (section 2) that correspond with each of the models in this section are as follows:

Models	Elements of Mixture	Fragments
1, 2	F♭	1
3, 4	F♭ D, C♭	2
5	C♭, B♭♭	3
6	F♭, E♭♭, D, C♭, B♭♭	4

MODELS 1–6

a. Mixture

The first four models contain elements of modal mixture. For practice, sing example 1a, with one of your colleagues singing 1b, and so on.

b. Enharmonic changes (chromatic modulation)

Models	Enharmonic Changes	Fragments
7a, a', a"	A♭ = G♯	5
	G♭ = F♯	
	D♭ = C♯	
7b, 7b'		6

MODEL 7

The motives of examples 7a, 7a', and 7a" represent different orderings of the same intervallic patterns: M2, m3 (or M6), and P4. Examples 7b and 7b' represent the pattern m2 and M3 (outlining a P4).

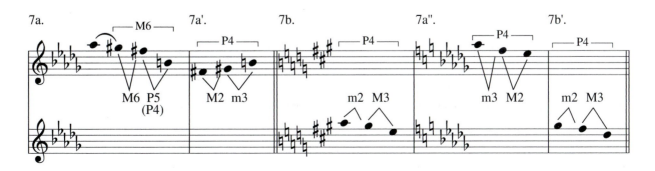

c. Motivic structure

Models	Fragments
8a	7a, 7b
8b	8a, 8b

MODEL 8

d. Chromatic and whole-tone models

Models	Fragments
9a, b, c, d	9

MODEL 9

These models are extracted from a highly chromatic song by Liszt. Altogether, these three motives (9a, b, and c) outline a whole-tone scale. Motive 9d represents a whole-tone scale.

e. Octatonic models

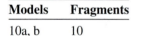

Models	Fragments
10a, b	10

MODEL 10

These models are extracted from Schoenberg's *Gurrelieder* (Songs of Gurre). Each pattern constitutes an *octatonic pentad*.

SECTION 2. Melodic Fragments—Intervals: All

Sing the following melodic fragments until you can sing them without error.

a. Mixture

1.

Del Tredici *The Acrostic Song* (Alice Pleasance Liddell) from *Final Alice* (transposed)

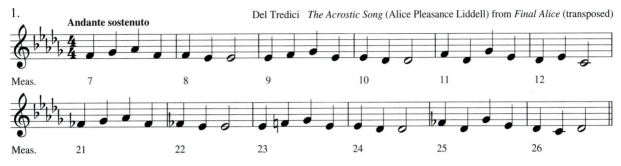

Meas.   7   8   9   10   11   12

Meas.   21   22   23   24   25   26

ACROSTIC SONG from FINAL ALICE (Del Tredici) © Copyright 1978 by Boosey & Hawkes, Inc. Reprinted by permission.

2.

Liszt *Der Hirt* (The Shepherd) (transposed) (abridged)

Meas.   20   21   22   23

Meas.   83   84   88   89

Liszt *Pace non trovo* (I Find No Peace) (Petrarch Sonnet) (transposed)

3.

Prokofiev *Sladkaya pesenka* (Sweet Melody), op. 68, no. 2

4.

Sweet Melody from *Three Children's Songs for Piano,* Op. 68 by Sergei Prokofiev. Copyright © 1946 (Renewed) by G. Schirmer, Inc. (ASCAP)
International Copyright Secured. All Rights Reserved. Reprinted by permission.

b. Modulation—enharmonic changes

Liszt *Der Fischerknabe* (The Fisher Lad)

5.

D♭M: AM:

6. **Allegretto, senza sientare**   enh.   Liszt *Der Fischerknabe*

AM: D♭M:

c. Motivic structure

7a. **Andante**   Brahms   Symphony no. 3, II (transposed)

7b. **Allegro energico**   Brahms   Ballade op. 118, no. 3 (transposed)

8a. **Langsam und leise**   Brahms   *Immer leiser wird mein Schlummer* (Fretful Slumber), op. 105, no. 2 (transposed)

8b. **Andante**   Brahms   Piano Concerto no. 2, op. 83, III (transposed)

d. Chromatic and whole tone

9. **Sehr langsam, sehnsuchtsvoll**   Liszt   *Mignon Lied* (Mignon's Song) (transposed)

e. Octatonic

10.   Schoenberg   *Gurrelieder* (Songs of Gurre), "Die wilde Jagd" (The Wild Chase) (octave lower).
Students are encouraged to alternate in the singing of motives a and b.

R-38

Rasch

SECTION 3. Creating a Coherent Melody

Return to section 2 and select two or three segments of melodic fragments that create a coherent melody. It may be necessary to change the meter and rhythm of certain segments, depending on your choice.

SECTION 4. Improvisation

1. Return to the "vocalise pattern" that was introduced in unit 7-B, section 4, and expand this pattern to incorporate elements of "mixture" through improvisation.

Vocalise pattern

Example of an improvised vocalise pattern with mixture

Choose one of the melodic fragments that illustrates "mixture" (1–4) as the basis for an improvisation.

2. Return to the "vocalise pattern" that was introduced in unit 7-B, section 4, and expand this pattern to incorporate an "enharmonic change" that results in a "chromatic modulation" through improvisation.

Vocalise pattern

Example of an improvised vocalise pattern with an enharmonic change (chromatic modulation)

Choose one of the melodic fragments that illustrates enharmonic change (chromatic modulation) (5–6) as the basis for an improvisation.

3. Return to the "vocalise pattern" that was introduced in Unit 7-B, section 4, and expand this pattern to incorporate a "motivic structure" that develops through improvisation.

Vocalise pattern

Example of an improvised vocalise pattern with a motivic structure that develops

Choose one of the melodic fragments that illustrates a motivic structure that develops (7–8) as the basis for an improvisation.

4. Return to the "vocalise pattern" that was introduced in unit 7-B, section 4, and expand this pattern to incorporate chromatic, whole-tone, or octatonic elements through improvisation.

Vocalise pattern

Example of an improvised vocalise pattern that incorporates chromatic, whole-tone, or octatonic elements through improvisation

Choose one of the melodic fragments (9–10) that illustrates chromatic, whole-tone, or octatonic elements as the basis for an improvisation.

C Twentieth-Century Cabaret Songs by Arnold Schoenberg

1.

Schoenberg *Der genügsame Liebhaber* (The Easily Satisfied Lover) (text by Hugo Salus) April, 1901

Used by permission of Belmont Music Publishers, Pacific Palisades, CA 90272

2. **Rasch**   Schoenberg *Jedem das Seine* (To Each His Own) (text by Colly) June, 1901

Langsamer *rit.*

a tempo
Rasch

Viel langsamer

Etwas langsamer

Rascher

rit. *rit.*

rit. *rit.* **Nicht zu langsam**

3. **Leicht bewegt**   Schoenberg   *Mahnung* (Warning) (text by Gustav Hochstetter) July, 1901

Used by permission of Belmont Music Publishers, Pacific Palisades, CA 90272

D Twentieth-Century Songs

SECTION 1. Art Songs by Ravel, Holst, and Carter

Ravel *Soupir* (Sigh), from *Trois Poèmes de Stéphane Mallarmé* (Three Poems of Stéphane Mallarmé), I (dedicated to Igor Stravinsky)

Soupir (Sigh), from *Trois Poèmes de Stéphane Mallarmé* (Three Poems of Stéphane Mallarmé), I (dedicated to Igor Stravinsky), *Maurice Ravel Songs 1896–1914,* edited by Arbie Orenstein. Copyright 1990 by Dover Publications, Inc. All rights reserved under Pan American and International Copyright Conventions.

Ravel *Placet futile* (Futile petition), from *Trois Poèmes de Stéphane Mallarmé,* II (dedicated to Florent Schmitt)

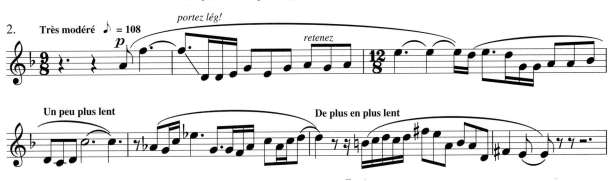

Placet futile (Futile petition), from *Trois Poèmes de Stéphane Mallarmé* (Three Poems of Stéphane Mallarmé), II (dedicated to Florent Schmitt), from *Maurice Ravel Songs 1896–1914,* edited by Arbie Orenstein. Copyright 1990 by Dover Publications, Inc. All rights reserved under Pan American and International Copyright Conventions.

Ravel   *Surgi de la croupe et du bond* (Riding from the Crupper and the Leap), from *Trois Poèmes de Stéphane Mallarmé,* III
(dedicated to Erik Satie)

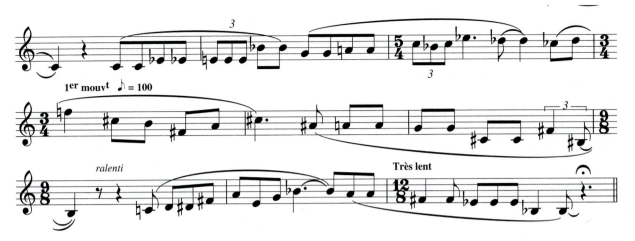

Surgi de la croupe et du bond (Riding from the Crupper and the Leap), from *Trois Poèmes de Stéphane Mallarmé* (Three Poems of Stéphane Mallarmé), III (dedicated to Erik Satie), *Maurice Ravel Songs 1896–1914,* edited by Arbie Orenstein. Copyright 1990 by Dover Publications, Inc. All rights reserved under Pan American and International Copyright Conventions.

Ravel   *Kaddisch* (Kaddish), from *Deux Mélodies Hébraïques* (Two Hebrew Melodies)

Kaddisch (Kaddish), from *Deux Mélodies Hébraïques* (Two Hebrew Melodies), *Maurice Ravel Songs 1896–1914,* edited by Arbie Orenstein.
Copyright 1990 by Dover Publications, Inc. All rights reserved under Pan American and International Copyright Conventions.

5. **Tranquillo** ♩ = 92   Ravel   *L'Enigme Eternelle* (The Eternal Enigma), from *Deux Mélodies Hébraïques*

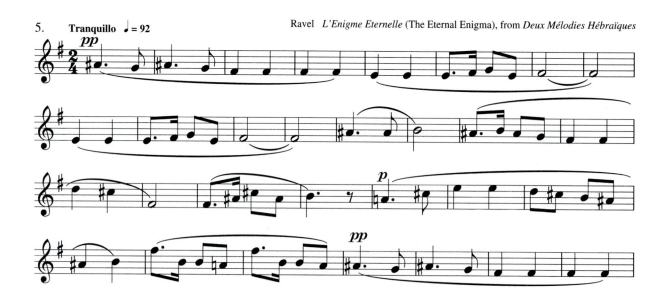

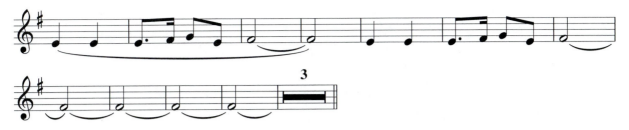

L'Enigme Eternelle (The Eternal Enigma), from *Deux Mélodies Hébraïques* (Two Hebrew Melodies), *Maurice Ravel Songs 1896–1914*, edited by Arbie Orenstein. Copyright 1990 by Dover Publications, Inc. All rights reserved under Pan American and International Copyright Conventions.

Holst *Persephone*

6. **Allegro**

Persephone, from *Twelve Humbert Wolfe Songs* by Gustav Holst. © 1930 by Augener, Ltd. Published by Galliard Ltd.

Elliott Carter "The Rose Family"

7. **Allegretto, con moto**

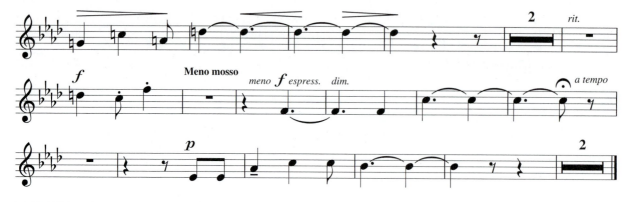

THE ROSE FAMILY from THREE FROST SONGS. By Elliot Carter and Robert Frost. Copyright © 1947 (Renewed) by Associated Music Publishers, Inc. (BMI). International Copyright Secured. All Rights Reserved. Reprinted by Permission.

SECTION 2. Melodies by Stravinsky (*Pastorale*) and Rossini (*Du séjour de la lumière* and *Sombre forêt*)

2. **Andantino**

PAMIRA

Cinti-Damoreau II

Adapted from *Du séjour de la lumiére* (From the Abode of Life) by Gioacchino Rossini and published in *Embellished Opera Arias,* edited by Austin B. Caswell. Recent Researches in the Music of the Nineteenth and Early Twentieth Centuries, vols. 7–8. Madison, Wisconsin: A-R Editions, Inc., 1989. Used with permission.

3. **Andantino** MATHILDE

Rossini *Sombre forêt* (Dark Forest), from *Guillaume Tell* (William Tell)

Based on *Sombre forêt* (Dark Forest) by Gioacchino Rossini and published in *Embellished Opera Arias,* edited by Austin B. Caswell. Recent Researches in the Music of the Nineteenth and Early Twentieth Centuries, vols. 7–8. Madison, Wisconsin: A-R Editions, Inc., 1989. Used with permission

E Ensembles

SECTION 1. Ensemble Singing in Familiar Clefs

Stravinsky *Perséphone*

En - core ___ mal ré - veil - lé - e Per - sé - pho - ne é - mer - veil - lé - e

Per - sé - pho - ne é - mer - veil - lé - e

Hors du si - nis - tre par - vis. Tu t'a - van - ces et comme i - vre de nuit

Hors du si - nis - tre par - vis. Tu t'a - van - ces et comme i - vre de nuit

Hors du si - nis - tre par - vis. Tu t'a - van - ces et comme i - vre de nuit

et comme i - vre de nuit

tu dou - tes de vi - vre En - co - re et pour - tant tu vis.

tu dou - tes de vi - vre En - co - re et pour - tant tu vis.

tu dou - tes de vi - vre En - co - re et pour - tant tu vis.

tu dou - tes de vi - vre En - co - re et pour - tant tu vis.

PERSÉPHONE (Stravinsky). © Copyright 1934 by Hawkes & Son (London) Ltd. Copyright Renewed. Revised version © Copyright 1950 by Hawkes & Son (London) Ltd. Copyright Renewed. Reprinted by permission of Boosey & Hawkes, Inc.

Schoenberg *Für Alban Berg zum 9. Februar 1935* written in honor of Alban Berg's 50th birthday

UNIT FIFTEEN

A Rhythm: Changing Meters

SECTION 1. Modules in Changing Meters

Consider each measure as a module to be practiced separately or as part of a continuous exercise. If the modules are treated as a continuous exercise, consider eighth notes as equivalent in simple meter, quarter as dotted quarter in compound, and so on.

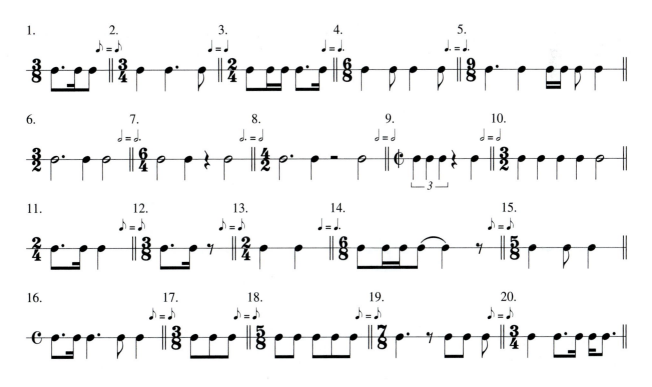

SECTION 2. Phrases in Changing Meters

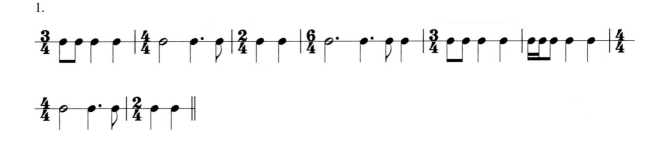

8.

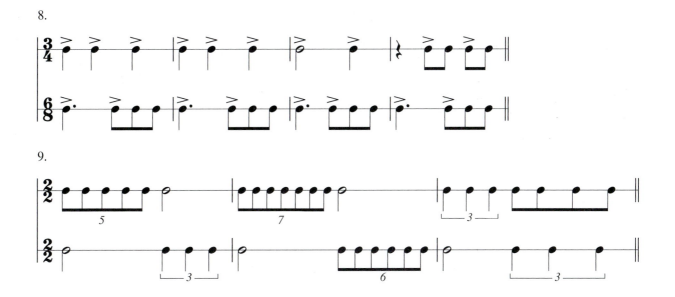

9.

SECTION 3. Creating a Coherent Phrase in Changing Meters

Return to section 1 and select three or four rhythm modules. Place the modules into a coherent four-measure phrase.

Write your solution on the following line:

B Atonal Models and Melodic Fragments for Interval Study—Intervals: All

SECTION 1. Atonal Models

I. The exercises in this section are atonal.

Within the atonal context, a few whole-tone and octatonic patterns are found. All exercises relate to the music of Strauss, Schoenberg, Debussy, and Bartók.

Each model in this section is related to the same corresponding number in the fragments. Each exercise has several segments (example 1: segments a–d) to encourage class participation by as many individuals as possible. One sings *a* while the next repeats *a* and continues with *b* and so on. For these atonal exercises, you should use whatever solfeggio or number system your instructor suggests.

MODELS 1-2

Model 1 focuses on the M6 and m2.

Model 2 is a study in 7ths.

MODELS 3 AND 4

Model 3 is based on a six-note pattern (later known as pitch-class set 6–Z4).

Sing the outer voices; the inner voices are provided to establish context.

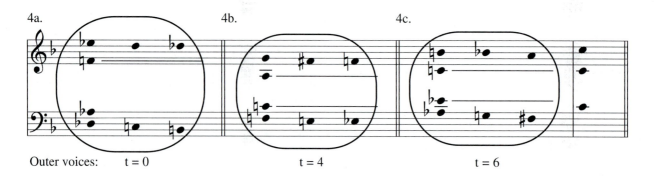

MODELS 5–10

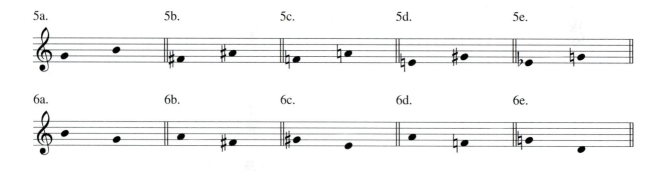

Models 7–10 should be sung in ensemble.

7a. 7b. 7c. 7d.

8a. 8b. 8c. 8d. 8e.

9a. 9b. 9c. 9d. 9e. 9f.

10a. 10b. 10c. 10d. 10e. 10f.

└──── Octatonic ────┘ └──── Octatonic ────┘ └──── Whole Tone ────┘

SECTION 2. Melodic Fragments—Intervals: All

R. Strauss   *Salome*, op. 54

1.
Andante mosso

Schoenberg   *Pelléas et Mélisande*, op. 5

2.
Etwas rascher

└─ t = 0 ─┘ └─ t = 2 ─┘ └─ t = 4 ─┘ └─ t = 6 ─┘ └─ t = 8 ─┘

Used by permission of Belmont Music Publishers, Pacific Palisades, CA 90272.

Schoenberg   *Pelléas et Mélisande*, op. 5

3.   **Langsamer werdend und abnehmend**

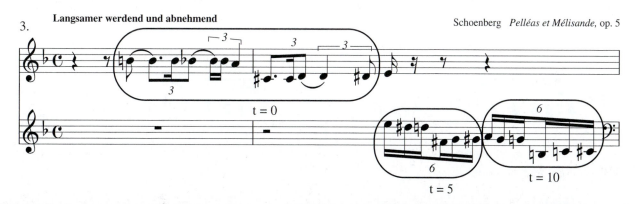

t = 0

t = 5

t = 10

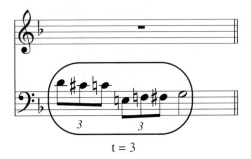

t = 3

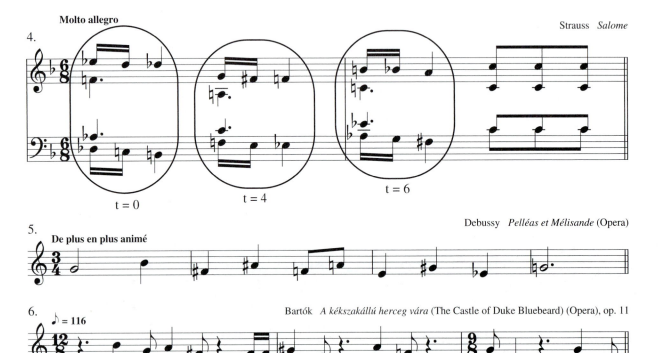

Strauss *Salome*

Molto allegro

4.

t = 0   t = 4   t = 6

Debussy *Pelléas et Mélisande* (Opera)

5. **De plus en plus animé**

6. ♪ = 116   Bartók *A kékszakállú herceg vára* (The Castle of Duke Bluebeard) (Opera), op. 11

Strauss *Salome*

7. **Più mosso**   3   3   3   3

8. **In gehender Bewegung**   Schoenberg *Pelléas et Mélisande*, op. 5

9.   Bartók *The Castle of Duke Bluebeard*, op. 11
Meno mosso

10.

SECTION 3. Creating a Coherent Melody

Return to section 2 and select two or three segments of melodic fragments that create a coherent melody. It may be necessary to change the meter and rhythm of certain segments, depending on your choice.

SECTION 4. Improvisation

Return to unit 14, part D, section 2 and review the vocalises by Stravinsky (*Pastorale*) and Rossini (*Du séjour de la lumière* [From the Abode of Life]). Notice that both of these examples are in major keys and emphasize raised scale degree 4 and lowered scale degree 7.

The two rhythmic reductions that follow are derived from the Stravinsky *Pastorale* (1) and the Rossini (*Du séjour de la lumière* [From the Abode of Life]) (2). Use these reductions as models for improvisations.

C Twentieth-Century Melodies for Careful Study and Preparation

This section contains works by Milhaud, Debussy, Menotti, Griffes, Bernstein, Weill, Trinkley, Barsom, and others.

Milhaud   *La Création du Monde* (The Creation of the World)

La Création du Monde Written by Darius Milhaud, © Editions Durand (SACEM). All rights for the world on behalf of Editions Durand (SACEM) administered by BMG Music Publishing France (SACEM). All rights for the U.S. on behalf of BMG Music Publishing France (SACEM) administered by BMG Songs, Inc. (ASCAP). Used by permission.

Milhaud   *La Création du Monde* (The Creation of the World)

2.

Flute

La Création du Monde Written by Darius Milhaud, © Editions Durand (SACEM). All rights for the world on behalf of Editions Durand (SACEM) administered by BMG Music Publishing France (SACEM). All rights for the U.S. on behalf of BMG Music Publishing France (SACEM) administered by BMG Songs, Inc. (ASCAP). Used by permission.

Santa Rosalia by Bruce Trinkley, based on the painting by Fernando Botero (libretto by Jason Charnesky)

3.

Oboe

Santa Rosalia. Copyright © 1994 Bruce Trinkley and J. Jason Charnesky.

Paul Barsom   "On Imminent Rays"

4.

Cello

5.

Debussy String Quartet op. 10, III

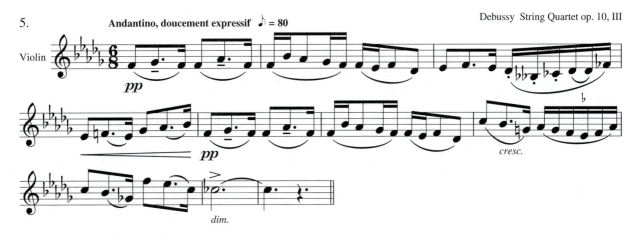

Debussy *Des pas sur la neige* (Footsteps in the Snow), Book I, Prelude VI

6.

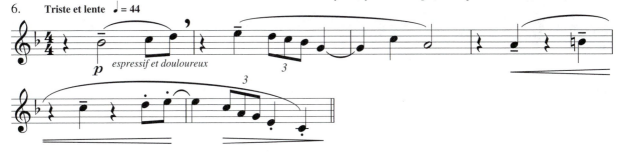

Debussy *La fille aux cheveux de lin* (The Girl with the Flaxen Hair), Book I, Prelude VIII

7.

Gian Carlo Menotti "The Black Swan" from *The Medium*

8.

9. Languidamente ♩ = 72–80   Charles T. Griffes *Symphony in Yellow*, op. 3, no. 2

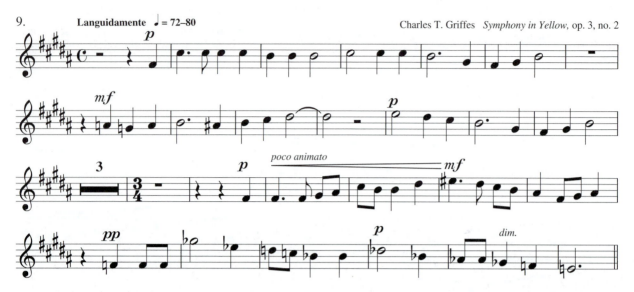

Leonard Bernstein   "It Must Be Me" (reprise of "It Must Be So") from *Candide*

10. Very slowly and freely, like a folk song

11.   Kurt Weill "The Lonesome Dove" from *Down in the Valley*

Moderato assai

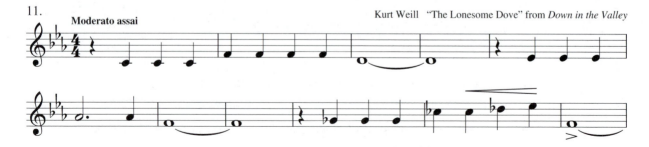

Paul Hindemith *Engelkonzert* (Angelic Concert) from *Symphonie Mathis der Maler*

12.

♩ = 108–112

(to be transposed down an 8ve)

Flute

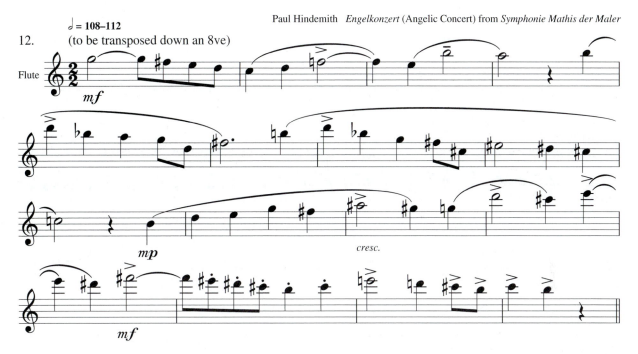

♩ = 108–112

(to be transposed down an 8ve)

Hindemith *Engelkonzert* (Angelic Concert) from *Symphonie Mathis der Maler*

13.

Flute

Kodály *Valsette*

14. Allegro (♩. = 80)

15.

Bartók   Bagatelle no. 1 from *Fourteen Bagatelles,* op. 6

Molto sostenuto ♩ = 66

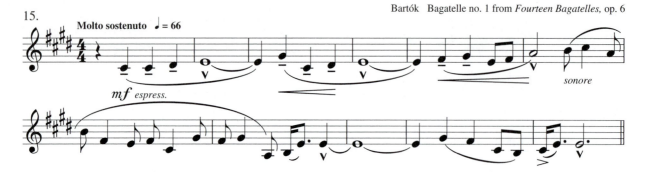

Bagatelle no. 1 from *Fourteen Bagatelles,* op. 6, by Béla Bartók. © 1909 by Rozsnyai Károly, Budapest. Copyright assigned 1950 to Editio Musica Budapest.

Presto ♩ = 108
(to be transposed down an 8ve)

16.

Bartók   Bagatelle no. 14 from *Fourteen Bagatelles,* op. 6

Bagatelle no. 14 from *Fourteen Bagatelles,* op. 6, by Béla Bartók. © 1909 by Rozsnyai Károly, Budapest. Copyright assigned 1950 to Editio Musica Budapest.

Munter. Schnelle Viertel
(to be transposed down an 8ve)

17.

Hindemith   *Kleine Klaviermusik* (Short Piano Music), no. 3

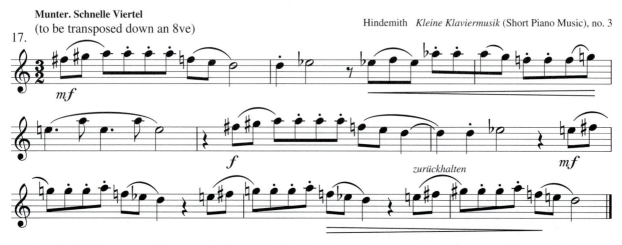

Hindemith KLEINE KLAVIERMUSIK, NO. 3 © 1929 by Schott Musik International, Mainz. © Renewed. All rights reserved. Used by permission of European American Distributors LLC, sole U.S. and Canadian agent for Schott Musik International, Mainz.

D   Vocalises by Honegger and Martinů

1.

Honegger   *Vocalise-étude*

♩ = 66

Reproduced with amiable authorization from Editions Alphonse Leduc-Paris.

Martinů *Vocalise-étude*

Reproduced with amiable authorization from Editions Alphonse Leduc-Paris.

E Ensembles of the Twentieth Century

SECTION 1. Ensemble Singing in Familiar Clefs

The following ensemble excerpts should be performed vocally, although instruments may be used to supplement voices. In addition to singing or playing parts in ensemble, you are encouraged to play entire excerpts at the keyboard.

PROCEDURE

1. Students should sing the melodic "reduction" of each excerpt, using whatever system is suggested by the instructor—solfege, numbers (1–8 or 0–11).

2. Students should take turns singing or playing individual lines of these excerpts before singing or playing them in ensemble.

3. Whenever possible, the instructor should bring recordings to class so that students will come to a full understanding of the musical context for each excerpt.

Examples 1 (Milhaud) and 2 (Hindemith) can be related to the melodic pattern, which encompasses six notes of the major scale:

1. From mi up to do (mi, fa, sol, la, ti, do), or
2. From 3 up to 1 (3, 4, 5, 6, 7, 1), or
3. From 4 up to 0 (4, 5, 7, 9, 11, 0)

1a.

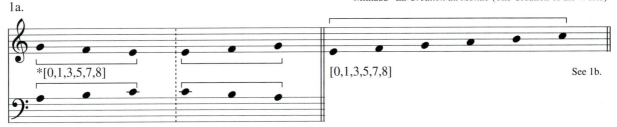

*[0,1,3,5,7,8]   [0,1,3,5,7,8]   See 1b.

Milhaud, *La Création du Monde* (The Creation of the World), (1923).

*For further explanation, see Allen Forte, *The Structure of Atonal Music.* New Haven, CT, Yale University Press, 1973.

Hindemith *Engelkonzert* (Angelic Concert), from *Symphonie Mathis der Maler*

2a.

[0,1,3,5,7,8]   [0,1,3,5,7,8]

See 2b.

Example 3 (Debussy) introduces a recurring four-note pattern (tetrachord) in the second violin part, which encompasses four notes of the major scale:

1.   From ti up to fa (ti, do, re, [mi], fa), or
2.   From 7 up to 4 (7, 1, 2, [3], 4), or
3.   From 11 up to 5 (11, 0, 2, [4], 5)

In the same example, the viola part has a recurring six-note pattern (hexachord), which can be thought of *at first* in two different tonalities:

1.   First three notes: do, ti, sol; last three notes: re, fa, sol
2.   First three notes: 1, 7, 5; last three notes: 2, 4, 5

Ultimately, students should be encouraged to think in terms of all twelve notes, with C being zero:

3.   7, 6, 2, 5, 8, 10

Whenever this six-note pattern is placed in "normal order" (see Forte's *Structure of Atonal Music*), the "pitch-class set" corresponds to 6-Z39 in Forte's taxonomy.

2, 5, 6, 7, 8, 10 and reduced to "zero level" (Forte)
0, 3, 4, 5, 6, 8 and inverted
0, 2, 3, 4, 5, 8

Debussy String Quartet op. 10, II (m. 10)

3a.   [0,1,3,6]

[0,2,3,4,5,8]

[0,3,4,5,6,8]

See 3b.

Example 4 (Debussy) features a three-note pattern in various transformations (cello). Although it is possible to think of each three-note pattern in its own tonality (la, do, si; do, si, ti), it is more beneficial for the student to recognize the pattern of alternating M3s and m3s, or alternating "interval classes" (Forte), which form [0,1,4]:

ic 3 (interval class three), encompassing three half-steps = m3
ic 4 (interval class four), encompassing four half-steps = M3
In combination, the first six notes of the cello part are entirely chromatic.

In the same part (cello) at the end of the first measure, the last five notes are a d7 chord: 0,3,6,9. Both of these melodic ideas are prominent in measure 19:

Melodically, [0,1,4] is found in all four parts.
Harmonically, [0,3,6,9] is found when all four parts are combined.

4a.

Debussy   String Quartet op. 10, IV (m. 15)

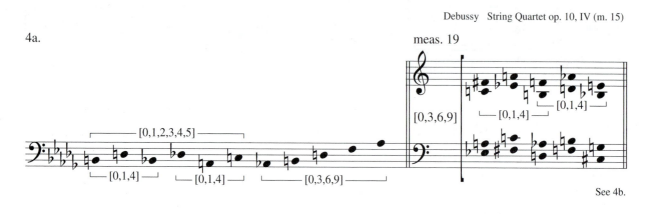

See 4b.

Example 5 (Hindemith) provides a wonderful opportunity for students to discover the sol, la, do, re pattern—sometimes referred to as the "I've Got Rhythm" tetrachord. The accompaniment is easily accessible for vocal or instrumental performance.

5a.   Hindemith   *Sing- und Spielmusiken* (Music to Sing and Play), from *Acht Kanons,* (Eight Canons), III, no. 2

See 5b.

1b.   Clarinet parts are written in B♭

Milhaud   *La Création du Monde* (The Creation of the World)

Hindemith MATHIS DER MALER © 1934 by Schott Musik International. © Renewed. Used by permission of European American Music Distributors LLC, sole U.S. and Canadian agent for Schott Musik International, Mainz.

3b.

Assez vif et bien rytmé ♩. = 112

4b.

En animant peu à peu ♩. = 108

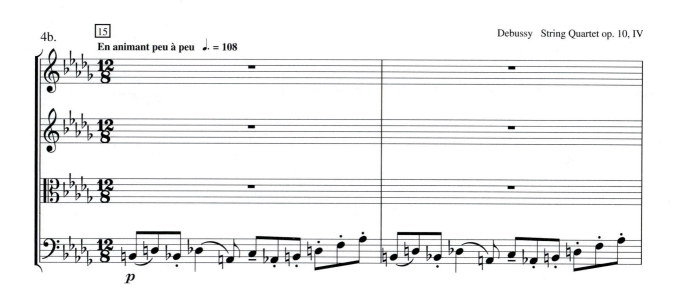

5b.

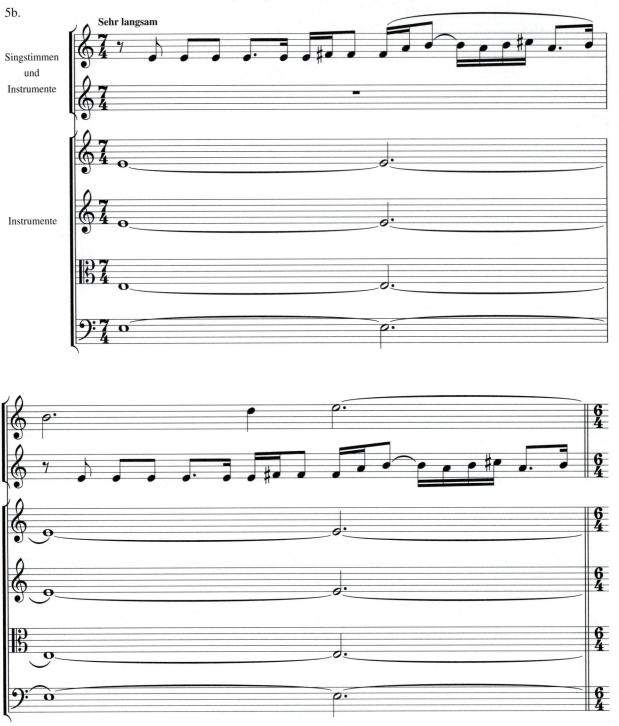

SECTION 2. Ensemble Singing in Unfamiliar Clefs

Genossenschaft
Deutscher Setzer
Ton-

Canon in 3 keys for the Genossenschaft Deutscher Tonsetzer, 5 parts

Deutscher Ton-

Genossenschaft

Setzer

Canon in Three Keys for the Genossenschaft Deutscher Tonsetze. Copyright © 1963 Bärenreiter-Verlag, Kassel. Reprinted by permission.

UNIT SIXTEEN

A Rhythm—Twentieth-Century Excerpt for Percussion

The entire class should participate in a reading of the opening bars of *Ionisation,* by Varèse.

Edgar Varèse *Ionisation*

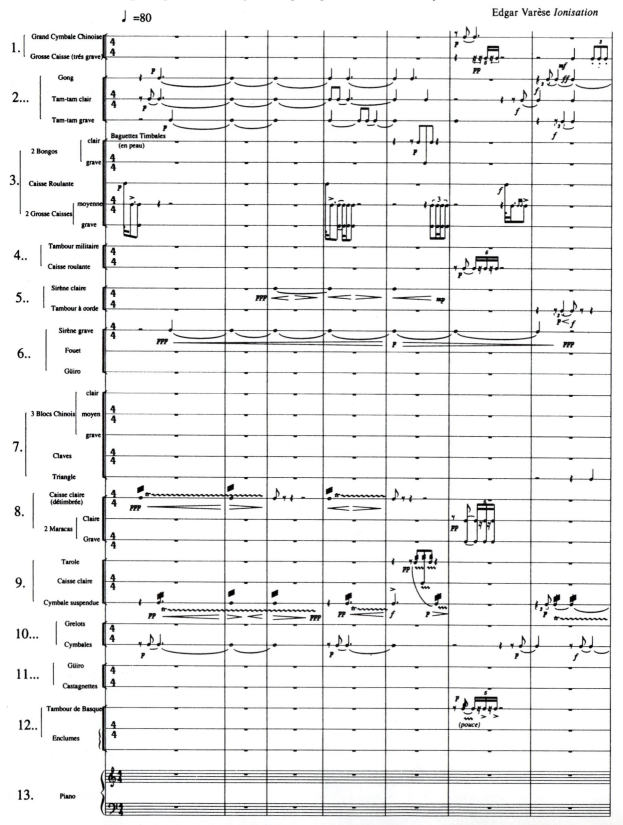

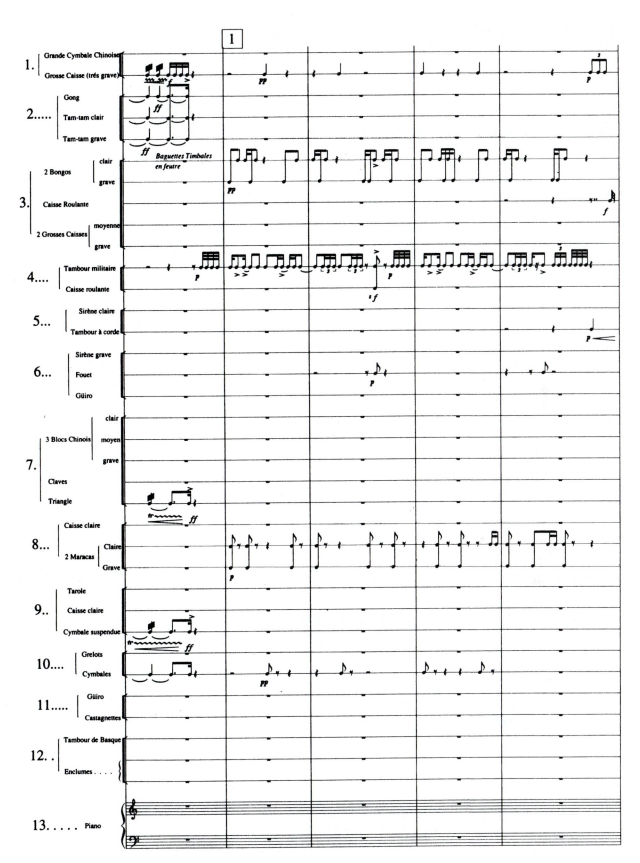

Ionisation Written by Edgard Varèse. © G. Ricordi & Co. (SIAE) All rights for the U.S. on behalf of G. Ricordi & Company (SIAE) administered by Careers-BMG Music Publishing, Inc. (BMI). Used by permission.

B Twelve-Tone Models and Melodic Fragments for Interval Study

SECTION 1. Models: Dyads, Trichords, Tetrachords, Pentachords, and Hexachords

All exercises in this section are of the 12-tone type and relate to the first example (only) in section 2. The format for building exercises for interval study is illustrated for the first exercise. By using this approach, all 20 of the excerpts in section 2 will be made much easier to accomplish.

To provide as much individual participation as possible, the following procedure is recommended for in-class practice. Divide the row into two-note patterns (dyads)—the last note of each new dyad becomes the first note of the next dyad. One class member begins by singing *a* and another sings *b* and so on. The repeated note also facilitates the practice of tossing dyads.

a. Dyads

The drill can be expanded to include three-note (trichord), four-note (tetrachord), five-note (pentachord), and six-note (hexachord) patterns. This system will help you "ease" into the singing of 12-tone melodies.

b. Trichords

c. Tetrachords

d. Pentachords

e. Hexachords

As you become more proficient, it should be possible to toss patterns at random. For some extra fun in class, one class member sings the first three notes and calls the name of another who, in turn, repeats the last pitch and the next three notes. You can continue this procedure through each of the 20 melodies in section 2. In the following illustration, class members request the size of the pattern (dyad, trichord, etc.) as they are calling the student's name.

SECTION 2. Melodic Fragments: 12-Tone Series

Each of the 20 melodies represents a 12-tone series, and all are excerpted from compositions by composers such as Schoenberg, Berg, and Webern. Most have been arranged to fit within a single voice range, and many have been rewritten in a rhythmic environment more suitable to vocal music.

Preparation for this assignment began earlier with the introduction of "Twelve-Tone Models and Melodic Fragments for Interval Study."

Assuming that your expertise improved with the gradually increasing difficulty of the models and fragments in previous chapters, you should find examples of these 12-tone series well within your mastery.

6.

7.

8.

9.

10.

11. All intervals

12. All intervals; modify to accommodate your voice

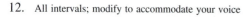

13.

14.

15.

16.

17.

18.

19.

20.

SECTION 3: Creating a Coherent Melody

Return to section 2 and select two or three segments of melodic fragments that would create a coherent melody. It may be necessary to change the meter and rhythm of certain segments, depending on your choice.

SECTION 4. Improvisation

Use the 12-tone series in example 11 of the previous section as the basis for improvisation.

C and D   Twentieth-Century Melodies for Careful Study and Preparation

Among the following melodies are works by Schoenberg, Berg, Webern, Stravinsky, Anderson, and Fenner.

1. Poco a poco sempre...più...come una pastorale

Berg   Violin Concerto, I (Carinthian Folk Tune)

2.

Berg   Violin Concerto, II, from *Es ist genug!* (It Is Enough), Bach Cantata 60

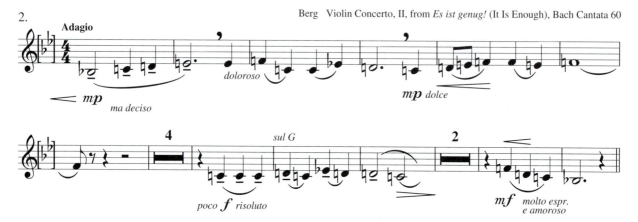

3.

Berg   Violin Concerto, II

4.

Schoenberg   *Verklärte Nacht* (Transfigured Night), op. 4

5.

6.

Webern   Passacaglia op. 1

Fenner   "The Sprightly Companion" for Oboe and Tape, III

7.

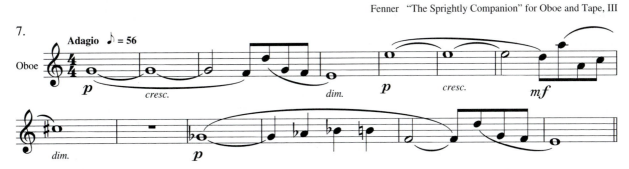

8.

T. J. Anderson   "Street Song"

9.

Stravinsky   *Symphonies of Wind Instruments*

10.

Berg *Wozzeck*

Marie

Stravinsky *Le sacre du printemps* (The Rite of Spring)

12.

Stravinsky *In Memoriam, Dylan Thomas*

Do not go gen-tle   in - to that good night,   Old age should burn and   rave at close of day;

Rage, rage a - gainst the dy   -   ing of the light . . . .

E Ensembles of the Twentieth Century

SECTION 1. Ensemble Singing in Familiar Clefs

The following ensemble excerpts should be performed vocally, although instruments may be used to supplement voices. In addition to singing or playing parts in ensemble, you are encouraged to play entire excerpts at the keyboard.

In example 1 (Fenner), the special charm of "The Sprightly Companion" is found in the symmetrical patterns of a nine-note scale: 0, 1, 2, 4, 5, 6, 8, 9, 10 in an imitative texture.

1a.

Fenner "The Sprightly Companion" for Oboe and Tape III

[0,1,2,   4,5,6   8,9,10]   See 1b.

Fenner "The Sprightly Companion" by Burt Fenner. Reprinted by permission of D. I. Music.

In example 2 (Schoenberg), the 12-tone series for the Quintet can be thought of as two hexachords: motives A and B.

2a.

Schoenberg Quintet op. 26, III

A   B

Used by permission of Belmont Music Publishers, Pacific Palisades, CA 90272.   See 2b.

In example 3 (Schoenberg), at least three significant tetrachords are audible in the Introduction to the Variations:

Measures 4 and 7 [0,3,6,9]—"the diminished 7th tetrachord"
Measure 6 [0,2,5,7]—"the sol, la, do, re" ("I've Got Rhythm") tetrachord
Measure 7 [0,3,4,7]—"the major-minor" tetrachord, or combinations of major and minor trichords

Schoenberg *Variations for Orchestra,* op. 31

3a.

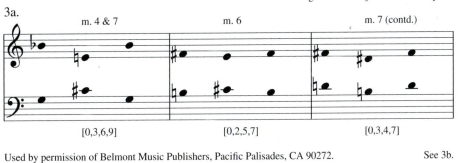

m. 4 & 7   m. 6   m. 7 (contd.)

[0,3,6,9]   [0,2,5,7]   [0,3,4,7]

Used by permission of Belmont Music Publishers, Pacific Palisades, CA 90272.   See 3b.

In example 4 (Schoenberg), all 12 tones are found in measures 122 and 123 (see 4b on page 337). This 12-tone piece can be used as a review of tetrachordal patterns.

Regarding example 5 (Anderson), in the composer's comment to Street Song, T. J. Anderson states: "Enculturation, the process of musically becoming, takes place for many people in children's game songs." This piece is based on a song that Mr. Anderson heard frequently while he was living in Atlanta, Georgia. The melody can be reduced to a six-note pattern:

E, D♯, E, C, A, G, C, D, C

In example 6, the atonal fugue (Berg) is based on a seven-note pattern. The vocal part, sung by Marie, depicts Mary Magdalene washing the feet of Jesus.

6a.

[0,1,2,3,4,5,7]   [0,1,2,3,4,5,7]   See 6b.

Example 7 (Stravinsky) is taken from *Threni*, Stravinsky's first work to be written entirely in the 12-tone serial technique. Notice that the excerpt gives two forms of the series: the original and the inversion.

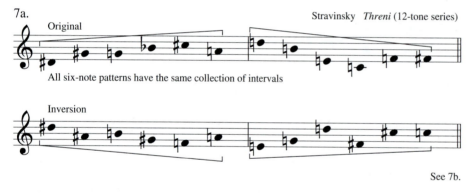

7a.   Stravinsky *Threni* (12-tone series)

Original

All six-note patterns have the same collection of intervals

Inversion

See 7b.

In example 8 (Stravinsky), the Carillon section of Stravinsky's *Firebird* (1910) has an elaborate atonal section, with multiple statements of a six-note pattern: [0,1,2,6,7,8] in the trumpet parts. As an experiment, students should transpose this pitch-class set at the tritone to see the order in which all six pitch classes will recur.

8a.   Stravinsky *Firebird*, R-99 (transposed to concert pitch)

[0,1,2,6,7,8]   [0,1,2,6,7,8]   [0,1,2,6,7,8]

See 8b.

In example 9 (Stravinsky), the closing measures of *Firebird* (1910) consist of a sequence of major triads in first inversion, which "harmonize" two different forms of the *Firebird* motive: [0,1,2,6].

. Stravinsky *Firebird* (closing measures)

9a.

See 9b.

In example 10 (Webern), the third of Webern's five canons consists of four motives, which are labeled as A (4-Z15), B (4–5), C (4–6), and D (4–4). The unity of this work is derived from the similarity among all of these motives, as indicated in the accompanying chart.

Webern *Five Canons*, op. 16, III

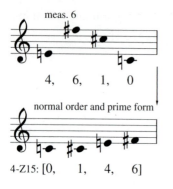

meas. 6

4, 6, 1, 0

normal order and prime form

4-Z15: [0, 1, 4, 6]

See 10b.

1b.

Fenner   "The Sprightly Companion" for Oboe and Tape, III

Fenner "The Sprightly Companion" by Burt Fenner. Reprinted by permission of D. I. Music.

It will not be necessary to transpose these instrumental parts since they are written in concert pitch.

2b.   Schoenberg *Bläserquintett* (Quintet for Wind Instruments), op. 26, III

Used by permission of Belmont Music Publishers, Pacific Palisades, CA 90272.

T. J. Anderson "Street Song"

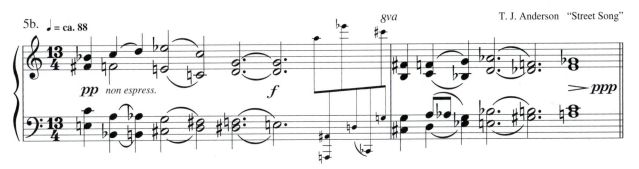

Berg *Wozzeck*, op. 7

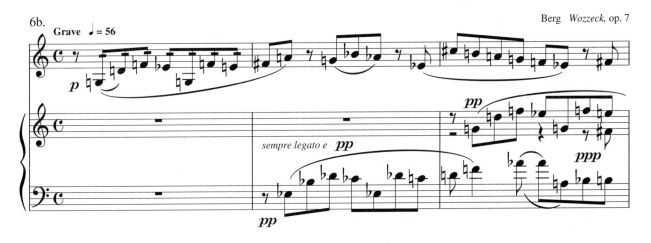

7b.

Stravinsky *Threni*

8b. Allegro ♩= 120

Stravinsky *L'oiseau de feu* (Firebird) (1910 Ballet)

Tpt. 1 in B♭ (senza sord.)

Tpt. 2 in B♭ (senza sord.)

Tpt. 3 in B♭ (senza sord.)

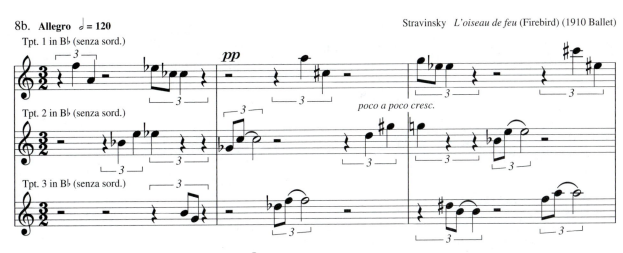

I.

II.

Tpt. 1, 2

9b.

Stravinsky *Firebird*

Molte pesante ♩= 60

Tpt. in A

From *Firebird Ballet*, Melodies 8 & 9. Reprinted by permission of J. & W. Chester, Ltd., London.

Webern *Five Canons*, op. 16, III

10b.

Langsam ♩= ca. 50

Crux   fi - de - lis,   in - ter

*Kl.

*Bkl.

om - nes   ar - bor   u - na   no - bi - lis:

nul - la   sil - va   ta - lem pro - fert,

* Clarinets sound at concert pitch

SECTION 2. Ensemble Singing in Unfamiliar Clefs

*(See example 2 in part C-D of this unit for reference to *Es ist genug* as a source for the second movement of Berg's Violin Concerto, II.)

Bach   *Es ist genug!* (It Is Enough), Chorale from Cantata 60*

Composer and Genre Index

Note: Translations for foreign titles appear on the indicated pages.

A

Afro-Cuban music
  batá drumming
    Ochún, 90, 92
    Oricha Oko, 127–128
Amish hymnody
  "Author of the Whole Creation," 28
  "Come Ye Sinners," 27
  "The Great Physician," 27
  "Jesus, Jesus, Source of Life," 27
  "Jesus, Lover of My Soul," 27
  "Praise God Forever," 28
  "Thousand Times by Me Be Greeted," 27
  "When the Due Time Had Taken Place," 28
Anderson, T. J., *Street Song,* 329, 337

B

Bach, Johann Sebastian
  Brandenburg Concerto (no. 2, I), 103
  Canon, *In dulci jubilo* (BWV 608), 121–122
  Cantatas
    (nos. 4, 5, 42, 46, 72), 135
    (nos. 75, 89, 144, 189, 197), 136
    no. 42, *Verleih' uns Frieden gnädiglich,* 61
  Chorale Cantata 26, *Ach wie nichtig, ach wie flüchtig,* 20
  Chorales
    (nos. 78, 126, 134, 170), 151
    (nos. 178, 172), 152
    Brunnquell aller Güter (BWV 445), 20
    Christe, der du bist Tag und Licht (BWV 274), 61
    Christus, der uns selig macht (BWV 283), 61
    Es ist genug! (from Cantata 60), 341–342
    Für Freuden laßt uns springen (BWV 313), 61
    Herr Gott, dich loben alle wir (BWV 328), 61
    Ich hab' dich einen Augenblick (Cantata 103), 248–249
    Ihr Gestirn', ihr hohlen Lüfte (BWV 476), 61
    Jesu, deine Liebeswunden (BWV 471), 20
    Meinen Jesum laß' ich nicht, weil (BWV 380), 61
    Nur mein Jesus ist mein Leben (BWV 490), 36
    Singt dem Herrn ein neues Lied (BWV 411), 61
  English Suite
    no. 3, *Gavotte* II, 103
    no. 5, *Gigue,* 132
  French Suite
    no. 3, *Sarabande,* 131
    no. 6, *Allemande,* 131
  Ich freue mich (BWV 465), 184
  Jesu, meines Glaubens (BWV 472), 184
  Die Kunst der Fuge
    Contrapunctus 5, 140
    Contrapunctus 13 (inversus), 139
    Contrapunctus 13 (rectus), 138
    no. 9, 131–132
    no. 12, rectus, inversus, 44
  Minuet I (BWV 841), 138
  Motet 3, *Jesu, meine Freude* (BWV 227), 122–124, 141–145
  Musikalisches Opfer (BWV 1079), 198, 217–218, 269–270
  Overture in F Major (BWV 820)
    Bourrée, 138
    Gigue, 138
    Trio, 138
  Partita no. 2, *Rondeau,* 131
  Partita no. 6, *Gavotte,* 130
  Sinfonia 13 (BWV 799), 7
  Der Tag mit seinem Lichte (BWV 448), 154–155
  Three-Part Invention (no. 2), 198
  Two-Part Invention (nos. 2, 4), 198
  Well-Tempered Clavier
    Book I, Fugue 4, 253
    Book I, Fugue 10, 131
    Book I, Fugue 24, 200
  Wie wohl ist mir, o Freund der Seelen (BWV 517), 154
  Wo ist mein Schäflein das ich liebe (BWV 507), 184
Barber, Samuel
  Bessie Bobtail (op. 2, no. 3), 104
  "I Hear an Army," 179
  Mélodies passàgeres (op. 27, no. 4), *Le clocher chante,* 205
  "Rain has Fallen," 181
  Vanessa, "Under the Willow Tree," 104
Barsom, Paul, "On Imminent Rays," 304–305
Bartók, Béla
  The Castle of Duke Bluebeard, op. 11, 302
  Fourteen Bagatelles, op. 6
    Bagatelle no. 1, 308
    Bagatelle no. 14, 308
Batá drumming. *See* Afro-Cuban music
Beethoven, Ludwig van
  (WoOs 191, 192, 193), 141
  (WoO 50), II, 140
  Feuerfarb' (op. 52, no. 2), 117
  Fidelio (op. 72c), Overture, 94
  Freundschaft (WoO 164), 191
  Das Glück der freundschaft (op. 88), 117
  Der Mann von Wort (op. 99), 117
  Missa Solemnis (op.123)
    Credo; Benedictus, 29
    Gloria, 28
  Piano Concerto (op. 73, no. 5, II), 114
  Piano Sonatas
    (op. 10, no. 1, I), 114
    (op. 10, no. 3, I), 131
    (op. 81a, II), 37

"'Tis the Last Rose of Summer," 207
"The Blackthorn Tree," 234
"A Bold Child," 228
"The Coulin" (lament), 6
"Da Luain, da Mairt," 77
"Derreen Day," 203
"The Fair Hills of E'ire O!", 232
"Farewell to Carraig An Eide," 206
"I Will Walk with My Love," 79
"Lillibulero," 80–81
"The Lone Rock," 231
"A New Song Called Granuaile," 79
"The Piper's Tunes," 79–80
"The Precious Treasure," 203
"The Soft Deal Board," 233
"Young Lad," 231
Irish sacred melodies
    Christmas Carol or Hymn, 209
    Funeral Cry, 209
    Irish Hymn Sung on the Dedication of a Chapel, 210
    Jesu dulcis memoria, 209

J

James, Harry. *See* Ellington, Duke
Jewish songs. *See also* Songs of the Babylonian Jews
    "Adon Olam," 55
    "Ets Chayim Hi," 56
    "Hasivenu Elecha," 57
    "Hevenu Shalom Aleychem," 54
    "Hin'ni Muchan Um'zuman," 55
    "L'cha Dodi," 55
    "Sim Shalom," 56–57
    "Yigdal," 55
    "Yismach Moshe," 56
Johnson, James Weldon, and Rosamund Johnson, *Lift Every Voice and Sing,* 267–269
Josquin des Prés. *See* Prés, Josquin des

K

Kodály, Zoltán
    Epigrams (Nine Vocalises), no. 1, 233
    Valsette, 307
Kurtz, Manny. *See* Ellington, Duke

L

Lasso, Orlando di
    "Beati quorum remissae sunt," 6
    Benedictus, 29–30
    Cantiones duarum vocum from *Fantasia III,* 45
    "Domine, ne in furore," 6
Lassus, Orlande de. *See* Lasso, Orlando di
Liszt, Franz
    Der Fischerknabe, 277–278
    Freudvoll und leidvoll, 253
    Der Hirt, 277
    Mignon Lied, 278
    Pace non trovo (Petrarch Sonnet), 277
    Die Vätergruft, 254

M

Machaut, Guillaume de
    Ballade no. 11 "N'en fait n'en dit n'en pensee," 87–88
    Hoquetus David, 108
    Tenor *David* (bass line), 95–96
Mahler, Gustav
    Das himmlische Leben, 241
    Kinder-Totenlieder, Nun will die Sonn' so hell aufgehn! (no. 1), 239
    Des Knaben Wunderhorn, Wer hat dies Liedlein erdacht, 95
    Das Lied von der Erde
        Das Trinklied vom Jammer der Erde, 238
        Der Abschied, 216–217
        Der Einsame im Herbst, 239
        Von der Jugend, 239
    Der Tamboursg'sell, 240
    Lieder eines fahrenden Gesellen
        Ging heut' Morgen über's Feld (no. 2), 240
        Wenn mein Schatz Hochzeit (no. 1), 240
Martinů, Bohuslav
    Kvet Broskví (Fleur du Pecher), 204
    Vocalise-étude, 309–310
McFarlane, Kathleen
    "Henry Morgan," 78
    "The Laughter of Raindrops," 77
Mendelssohn, Felix
    Songs Without Words
        Belief (op. 102, no. 6), 190
        Consolation (op. 30, no. 3), 188
        Elegy (op. 85, no. 4), 189
        The Fleecy Cloud (op. 53, no. 2), 189
        May Breezes (op. 62, no. 1), 189
        Retrospection (op. 102, no. 2), 190
        Sadness of Soul (op. 53, no. 4), 189
        Spring Song (op. 62, no. 6), 189
        Tarantella (op. 102, no. 3), 190
        Venetian Gondola Song (op. 30, no. 6), 188–189
Menotti, Gian Carlo, "The Black Swan," from *The Medium,* 305
Milhaud, Darius
    La Création du Monde, 303–304, 311, 312
    Vocalise étude, 229–230
Mills, Irving. *See* Ellington, Duke
Mozart, Wolfgang Amadeus
    adapted from song by Charles E. Graaf, basis for Eight Variations (K Anh. 208), 7
    adapted from "Ah, voud dirai-je, Maman," basis for 12 Variations (K.265/300e), 7
    "La belle Françoise," 21
    Canons
        Selig, selig, alle, alle (K.230/K.382b), 166–167
        Sie, sie dahin (K.229/K.382a), 168–173
    La Clemenza di Tito, 224
    Così fan Tutte, Terzettino: Soave sia il vento (K.588), no.10, 163–165
    Eight Minuets (K.315g), 36, 37
    Eight Variations, no. 8 (K.613), 21
    Die Entführung aus dem Serail, 226
    La finta giardiniera, 224, 225
    German Dance no. 5 (K.509), 21
    Horn Concerto (K.447)
        I, 113
        II, III, 114

Horn Concerto (K.495), I, 114, 150
Horn Concerto (K.417), III, 151
Idomeneo, act I, Aria (Electra), 50, 51
Eine kleine Nachtmusik (K.525), 50, 113
The Magic Flute (Die Zauberflöte)
   Duet Pamina, Papageno, 52
   no. 2, Lied (act I), 115
   no. 4, Recitative and Aria (act I), 115
   no. 8, Finale (act I), 115, 223
Minuet no. 2 (K.2), 94
Les noces de Figaro, 224–225
Piano Sonata (K.282/189g), I, 37
Requiem (K.626)
   Lacrymosa, 94
   Sanctus, 21
   Tuba Mirum, 94
Six German Dances (K.509), no. v, 95
Songs
   Abendempfindung (K.523), 160
   An Chloe (K.524), 159
   Dans un Bois Solitaire (K.308/295b), 155
   An die Einsamkeit (K.391/340b), 156
   Gesellenreise (Freimaurerlied) (K.468), 156, 157–158
   Im Frühlingsanfang (K.597), 158–159
   Das Kinderspiel (K.598), 157
   Des kleinen Friedrichs Geburtstag (K.529), 156
   Un moto di Gioja (K.579), 155, 159
   O Heiliges Band (der Freundschaft) (K.148/125h), 155
   Sehnsucht nach dem Frülinge (K.596), 158
   Die Verschweigung (K.518), 156, 159–160
   Warnung (K.433/416c), 157
   Die Zufriedenheit (K.349/367a), 156
   Die Zufriedenheit (K.473), 158
   Die Zufriedenheit im Niedrigen Stande (K.151/125f), 155
   Zum Schluss (K.484), 156
String Quartet (K.458), I, 107
Theme and Two Variations (K.460/454a), 21
Twelve Variations (K.179/189a), var. 8, 37
Variations on a Minuet by Duport (K.573), theme, 36
Muset, Colin. *See* Trouvéres, songs of
Mussorgsky, Modest
   Boris Godunov
      act 1, scene 1, 180
      "Polonaise," 232
      scene 2, 94

N

Negro Spiritual, *Deep River,* 208
Nemo, Henry. *See* Ellington, Duke

P

Pergolesi, Giovanni B.
   Adriano in Syria, Aria *Contento forse vivere nel mio martir potrei,* 161–162
   La Serva Padrona (act I, Aria), 135
Perkins, Frank. *See* Calloway, Cab
Prés, Josquin des, *Missa De Beata Virgine, Kyrie eleison,* 44
Primrose, Joe, "St. James Infirmary," 76–77
Prokofiev, Serge, *Sladkaya pesenka* (op. 68, no. 2), 277
Puccini, Giacomo, *Gianni Schicchi,* 134
Purcell, Henry, *King Arthur,* Frost scene, 226

R

Rameau, Jean-Philippe, *Les Indes galantes,* 160–161
Ravel, Maurice
   Deux Mélodies Hébraïques
      "Kaddisch," 287–288
      "L' Enigme Eternelle," 288–289
   Trois Poèmes de Stéphane Mallarmé
      "Placet futile" (no. 2), 285–286
      "Soupir" (no. 1), 285
      "Surgi de la croupe et du bond" (no. 3), 286–287
Redmond, John. *See* Ellington, Duke
Richard the Lion-hearted. *See* Trouvéres, songs of
Rossini, Gioacchino
   La siège de Corinthe, "Du séjour de la lumiere," 291–292
   Guillaume Tell
      Overture, 103
      "Sombre forêt," 293

S

Santería music. *See* Afro-Cuban music
Schoenberg, Arnold
   Bläserquintett, op. 26, III, 331, 335
   Canon 23, 270–271
   Chamber Symphony, op. 9, 329
   Für Alban Berg zum 9, Februar 1935, 295–296
   Der genügsame Liebhaber, 280–281
   Gurrelieder, "Die wilde Jagd," 278
   Genossenschaft Deutscher Tonsetzer, Canon in 3 keys and 5 parts for, 319–321
   Jedem das Seine, 281–283
   Mahnung, 283–284
   Pelléas et Mélisande, op. 5, 301–302, 302
   Quintet, op. 26, III, 331, 335
   String Trio, op. 45, 337
   Variations for Orchestra, op. 31, 331, 336
   Verklärte Nacht, op. 4, 328
Schubert, Franz
   Am Flusse (D.766), 58
   Am Meer, 254
   Der Atlas, 254
   Der Doppelgänger, 253
   Drang in die Ferne (D.770), 59
   Ecossaise I (D.421), 103
   Ihr Bild, 181
   Liebe säuseln die Blätter (D.988), 242–245
   Der Musensohn (D.764a), 59
   Die schöne Müllerin (D.795), "Die böse Farbe," no. 17, 238
   Schwanengesang (D.318), no. 5, "Aufenthalt," 58
   Schweizerlied (D.559), 58
   Symphony no. 5, Minuet, 50, 51
   Symphony no. 8 ("Unfinished") (D.759), I, 60
   Variation on a Waltz by Diabelli (D.718), 95
   Winterreise (op.89, D.911)
      Einsamkeit (no. 12), 236
      Estarrung (no. 4), 58
      Im Dorfe (no. 17), 237
      Der Leiermann (no. 24), 59
      Der Lindenbaum (no. 5), 59
      Die Post (no. 13), 236
      Rast (no. 10), 235
      Rückblick (no. 8), 235

Der Stürmische (no. 18), 237
Täuschung (no. 19) 237
Wasserflut (no. 6), 235
Das Wirtshaus (no. 21), 237–238
Zwei Szenen aus "Lacrimas" (op.124, no. 1, D.857 [2]), II
(Delphine), 59
Schumann, Clara
Ich hab' in deinem Auge (op. 13, no. 5), 185–186
Piano Trio, 186
Three songs (op. 12, Rückert)
Er ist gekommen in Sturm und Regen (no. 2), 185
Liebst du um Schönheit (no. 4), 185
Warum willst du andre fragen? (no. 11), 185
Was weinst du, Blümlein (op. 23, no. 1), 186
Schumann, Robert
Album for the Young
Ernteliedchen (op. 68, no. 24), 102
Kleine Romanze (op. 68, no. 19), 102
Schnitterliedchen (op. 68, no. 18), 102
Stückchen (op. 68, no. 5), 101–102
Trällerliedchen (op. 68, no. 3), 101
Wilder Reiter (op. 68, no. 8), 101
Albumblätter, #5, 102
Der Hidalgo (op. 30, no. 3), 187
Nichts Schöneres (op. 36, no. 3), 188
Papillons (op. 2, nos. 3, 12), 101
Scherzo (op. 99, no. 13), 102
Stille Thränen (op. 35, no. 10), 188
Stirb, Lieb' und Freud! (op. 35, no. 2), 187
Was soll ich sagen (op. 27, no. 3), 187
Widmung (op. 25, no. 1), 186
Schütz, Heinrich, *Die sieben Worte Jesu Christi, Introitus,*
246–247
Smith, Chris
"Ballin' the Jack," 255–256
"Boom, Tum, Ta-Ra-Ra—Zing Boom!," 256–257
Songs of the Babylonian Jews, Idelsohn Collection
hôdu—Passover, 6
im afês—Selihot, 6
Stewart, Rex. *See* Ellington, Duke
Strauss, Richard, *Salome,* op. 54, 301, 302
Stravinsky, Igor
Berceuse, 230
Firebird, R-99, 332, 333, 339
Histoire pour enfants, Timlimbom, (no. 1), 202–203
Le sacre du printemps, 330
In Memoriam, Dylan Thomas, 330
Pastorale, 290
Perséphone, 294
Petrouchka, 131, 180
Quatre Chants Russes
Canarde (Ronde) (no. 1), 206
Chanson pour compter (no. 2), 205
Symphonies of Wind Instruments, 329
Threni, 332, 338
Strayhorn, Billy, and Delta Rhythm Boys, "Take the
'A' Train," 263. *See also* Ellington, Duke

T

Tchaikovsky, Pyotr, Symphony no. 5 (op. 64), 95
Telemann, Georg Philipp, *Fuga 2,* 191–192
Thibault IV, King of Navarre. *See* Trouvéres, songs of
Trinkley, Bruce, *Santa Rosalia,* 304
Troubador songs. *See* Trouvéres, songs of
Trouvéres, songs of
"Chanson de croisade" no. 326 (Lord of Couch), 98
"Chanson" no. 108 (Colin Muset), 201
"Chanson" no. 112 (Adam de la Hale), 99
"Chanson" no. 152 (Richard the Lion-hearted), 99
"Chanson" nos. 59-60 (Gace Brulé), 99–100
"Pastorelle" no. 142 (Thibaut IV, King of Navarre), 98
"Reverdie" no. 5 (Gace Brulé), 202

V

Varèse, Edgar, *Ionisation,* 322–323
Verdi, Guiseppe
Aida
(act IV), 130
Duet Aida and Amonasro (act III), 134
Duet Aida and Radames (act III), 134
Attila (act II), 134, 135
Nabucco
Chorus of the Hebrew Slaves, 133
Chorus of the Levites, 133
Mio furor, non più costretto, 133

W

Wagner, Richard
Die fliegende Holländer, Overture, 50, 51
Götterdämmerung
act III, 179
scene 3, 180
scenes 1,2, 200
scenes 1-3, 130
Prelude, 200
Webern, Anton
Five Canons, op. 16, III, 333–334, 339–340
Passacaglia, op. 1, 329
Webster, Paul. *See* Ellington, Duke
Weill, Kurt, "The Lonesome Dove" from *Down in the Valley,*
306–307
Wilder, Alec, *Five Vocalises*
no. 1, 259–260
no. 2, 260
no. 3, 261
no. 4, 261–262
no. 5, 262